Contents

Valentine's Day Cake

Easy Flourless Chocolate Cake

Prep: 15 mins **Cook:** 1 hr 5 mins **Additional:** 9 hrs **Total:** 10 hrs 20 mins

Servings: 12

Yield: 1 10-inch cake

Ingredients

- 1 teaspoon vegetable oil
- 15 ounces semisweet chocolate morsels
- 15 ounces unsalted butter
- 1 ¾ cups white sugar
- 10 eaches eggs
- ¼ cup water
- 2 teaspoons vanilla extract

Directions

Step 1

Preheat oven to 325 degrees F (165 degrees C). Grease a 10-inch cake pan with oil.

Step 2

Combine chocolate, butter, and sugar in a double boiler over simmering water; cook, stirring frequently and scraping down the sides with a rubber spatula, until melted and smooth, about 5 minutes.

Step 3

Pour chocolate mixture into the bowl of a stand mixer fitted with the paddle attachment; beat on low speed until cooled, about 5 minutes. Increase speed to medium; beat in eggs one at a time. Add water and vanilla extract; beat on low speed until blended. Pour into the prepared pan.

Step 4

Place cake pan inside a large baking dish. Pour enough water into the baking dish to come halfway up the sides of the cake pan.

Step 5

Bake cake in the preheated oven until a knife inserted into the center comes out clean, about 1 hour. Allow cake to cool in the water bath, about 1 hour. Transfer to the refrigerator; chill until firm, 8 hours to overnight.

Nutrition Facts

Per Serving:

597 calories; protein 7.4g 15% DV; carbohydrates 49.6g 16% DV; fat 43.7g 67% DV; cholesterol 211.7mg 71% DV; sodium 55.4mg 2% DV.

Heart Cake

Prep: 1 hr **Cook:** 45 mins **Additional:** 1 hr **Total:** 2 hrs 45 mins

Servings: 8

Yield: 10 servings

Ingredients

- ½ cup unsalted butter
- 1 tablespoon unsalted butter
- ⅔ cup white sugar
- 1 teaspoon vanilla sugar
- 4 large eggs eggs
- 5 ounces dark chocolate, chopped
- 1 ½ cups almond meal
- ¼ cup dry bread crumbs

Ganache:

- 5 ounces 70% dark chocolate, broken into small pieces
- ¾ cup confectioners' sugar
- ½ cup unsalted butter
- 2 tablespoons unsalted butter
- 3 drops almond extract

Decoration:

- 1 (4 ounce) package red marzipan
- 2 tablespoons assorted candy decorations, such as pink hearts, silver balls, etc.

Directions

Step 1

Preheat oven to 350 degrees F (175 degrees C). Grease a 9-inch heart-shaped pan with butter and dust with some extra bread crumbs.

Step 2

Cream 1/2 cup plus 1 tablespoon butter in a bowl with an electric mixer; mix in 2/3 cup white sugar and vanilla sugar. Add eggs one at a time, beating well after each addition, until light and foamy.

Step 3

Place 5 ounces chocolate in top of a double boiler over simmering water. Stir frequently, scraping down the sides with a rubber spatula to avoid scorching, until chocolate is melted, about 5 minutes. Cool for a few minutes, then blend into egg mixture. Mix almond meal with bread crumbs and fold into the chocolate batter. Pour batter into the prepared pan.

Step 4

Bake in the preheated oven on the lowest rack for 45 minutes. Remove from oven and cook completely, about 1 hour. Remove from pan.

Step 5

Place 5 ounces chocolate in top of a double boiler over simmering water. Stir frequently, scraping down the sides with a rubber spatula to avoid scorching, until chocolate is melted, about 5 minutes. Cool for a few minutes, then mix in confectioner's sugar.

Step 6

Cream 1/2 cup plus 2 tablespoons butter in a bowl with an electric mixer until creamy. Stir in chocolate-sugar mixture and almond extract until ganache is smooth.

Step 7

Cut heart cake horizontally into 2 layers. Cover the bottom layer with some chocolate ganache and place second layer on top. Cover heart on all sides with remaining chocolate ganache.

Step 8

Roll out marzipan into a thin layer on parchment paper. Cut out circles with a small glass to make petals; you need about 12 petals per rose. Roll one of the circles into a spiral shape for the center of the rose. Add the next marzipan circle and roll it around the center piece. The marzipan should just stick together. If you need extra "glue", use some water. Decorate cake with pink roses and other candy to your liking.

Cook's Note:

If you can't find red marzipan, just buy regular marzipan and color it yourself with a few drops of red food coloring.

Nutrition Facts

Per Serving:

745 calories; protein 15.2g 30% DV; carbohydrates 68.5g 22% DV; fat 48.3g 74% DV; cholesterol 167.2mg 56% DV; sodium 69.1mg 3% DV.

White Chocolate Strawberry Cake

Prep: 45 mins **Cook:** 30 mins **Total:** 1 hr 15 mins

Servings: 16

Yield: 16 servings

Ingredients

- 2 ¾ cups cake flour
- 2 ½ teaspoons baking powder
- 2 cups white sugar
- 1 cup butter, softened
- 1 (3 ounce) package strawberry flavored Jell-O
- 4 large eggs eggs
- 1 cup milk
- 1 teaspoon vanilla extract
- ½ cup strawberries, pureed
- 4 ounces cream cheese
- 4 ounces white chocolate baking squares
- 3 tablespoons heavy whipping cream
- 4 cups confectioners' sugar

Directions

Step 1

Preheat oven to 350 degrees F (175 degrees C).

Step 2

Grease two 9-inch round cake pans and line with waxed paper.

Step 3

Mix flour and baking powder in a bowl.

Step 4

Beat white sugar, butter, and gelatin together in a separate bowl until fluffy; add eggs, one at a time, beating well with each addition.

Step 5

Stir alternately flour mixture then milk, into sugar mixture to form a smooth batter. Stir vanilla extract and strawberries into batter until combined.

Step 6

Divide batter between prepared cake pans.

Step 7

Bake in the preheated oven until a toothpick inserted into the center of both cakes comes out clean, 25 to 30 minutes; cool completely.

Step 8

Stir cream cheese, white chocolate, and heavy whipping cream in a saucepan over medium heat until combined and white chocolate is melted, about 5 minutes.

Step 9

Stir confectioners' sugar into cream cheese mixture until a smooth frosting forms. Allow to cool and set.

Step 10

Spread a layer of frosting over the top of one cake. Place the second cake on top of frosting layer. Frost the top of second cake and sides of both cakes with remaining frosting.

Nutrition Facts

Per Serving:

524 calories; protein 5.7g 11% DV; carbohydrates 85.8g 28% DV; fat 18.5g 29% DV; cholesterol 89.4mg 30% DV; sodium 231.8mg 9% DV.

Extreme Chocolate Lover's Cake

Prep: 25 mins **Cook:** 35 mins **Total:** 1 hr

Servings: 16

Yield: 1 - 2 layer 9 inch cake

Ingredients

Cake:

- 2 ¼ cups all-purpose flour
- 2 teaspoons baking soda
- ½ teaspoon salt
- 6 (1 ounce) squares unsweetened chocolate, chopped
- ½ cup unsalted butter
- 2 ½ cups dark brown sugar
- 3 large eggs eggs
- 1 ½ teaspoons vanilla extract
- 1 cup sour cream
- 1 cup water

Frosting:

- 6 (1 ounce) squares unsweetened chocolate, chopped
- ¼ cup unsalted butter
- 1 egg yolk
- 4 cups confectioners' sugar
- 2 tablespoons vanilla extract
- 2 tablespoons heavy cream
- 1 (8 ounce) package cream cheese, softened

GANACHE:

- 2 cups bittersweet chocolate chips
- 1 cup heavy cream

Directions

Step 1

Preheat oven to 350 degrees F (175 degrees C). Grease and flour two 9-inch pans. Sift together the flour, baking soda and salt. Set aside. In the top of a double boiler, heat 6 ounces chocolate, stirring occasionally, until chocolate is melted and smooth. Remove from heat and allow to cool to lukewarm.

Step 2

In a large bowl, cream together the butter and brown sugar until light and fluffy. Beat in the eggs one at a time, then stir in 1 1/2 teaspoons vanilla. Stir in the melted chocolate. Beat in the flour mixture alternately with the sour cream. Stir in boiling water (batter will be thin). Pour batter into prepared pans.

Step 3

Bake in the preheated oven for 35 to 40 minutes, or until a toothpick inserted into the center of the cake comes out clean. Let cool in pan for 10 minutes, then turn out onto a wire rack and cool completely.

Step 4

Make the Chocolate Buttercream Frosting: In the top of a double boiler, heat 6 ounces chocolate, stirring occasionally, until chocolate is melted and smooth. Remove from heat and allow to cool to lukewarm. In a large bowl, whip the butter for about 10 minutes until it is super fluffy, beat in egg yolk. Gradually blend in the confectioners' sugar, alternating with 2 tablespoons vanilla and 2 tablespoons cream, then blend in the melted chocolate. Beat in the softened cream cheese.

Step 5

Make the Ganache: In a large saucepan, combine chocolate chips and 1 cup heavy cream. Heat, stirring constantly, until chocolate is melted and smooth. Remove from heat and set aside.

Step 6

Assemble the cake: When cake is completely cooled, cover the bottom cake layer with as much ganache as desired. Refrigerate for 5 minutes, or until ganache has set. Spread frosting over the ganache. Cover with top layer of cake. Frost top and sides with buttercream, and garnish with more ganache.

Nutrition Facts

Per Serving:

759 calories; protein 8.9g 18% DV; carbohydrates 100.9g 33% DV; fat 40.7g 63% DV; cholesterol 115.2mg 38% DV; sodium 321.7mg 13% DV.

Cherry Glazed Sponge Cake

Prep: 10 mins **Cook:** 45 mins **Total:** 55 mins

Servings: 20

Yield: 1 - 10x15 inch jellyroll pan

Ingredients

- 1 cup margarine
- 1 ½ cups white sugar
- 4 large eggs eggs
- 1 teaspoon almond extract
- 2 cups all-purpose flour
- 1 (21 ounce) can cherry pie filling
- 2 tablespoons confectioners' sugar for dusting

Directions

Step 1

Preheat oven to 350 degrees F (175 degrees C). Grease and flour a 10x15 inch jellyroll pan.

Step 2

In a large bowl, cream together the margarine and sugar until light and fluffy. Beat in eggs, one at a time, then stir in almond extract. Fold in flour until just blended. Spread batter into prepared pan. With the tip of a knife, mark squares in the batter. Spoon equal portions of pie filling in the center of each square.

Step 3

Bake in preheated oven for 35 to 40 minutes, or until golden brown, and a toothpick inserted into the center comes out clean. Allow to cool, then dust with confectioners' sugar.

Nutrition Facts

Per Serving:

236 calories; protein 2.8g 6% DV; carbohydrates 33.8g 11% DV; fat 10.1g 16% DV; cholesterol 37.2mg 12% DV; sodium 124.8mg 5% DV.

Easy Valentine's Day Cake

Prep: 30 mins **Cook:** 30 mins **Additional:** 2 hrs **Total:** 3 hrs

Servings: 16

Yield: 1 double-layer 8x8-inch cake

Ingredients

Cake:

- 2 cups white sugar
- 1 cup butter, softened
- 4 large eggs eggs, beaten
- 1 tablespoon vanilla extract
- 1 teaspoon almond extract
- 2 teaspoons baking powder
- 1 teaspoon baking soda
- 3 cups all-purpose flour
- 2 cups milk

Icing:

- 4 cups confectioners' sugar
- 1 cup butter, softened
- 2 teaspoons vanilla extract

Directions

Step 1

Preheat oven to 350 degrees F (175 degrees C). Grease an 8x8-inch square pan and an 8-inch round pan.

Step 2

Beat white sugar and 1 cup butter together in a bowl with an electric mixer until creamy and smooth. Mix eggs, 1 tablespoon vanilla extract, and almond extract into creamed butter mixture. Stir baking powder and baking soda into butter mixture until just combined.

Step 3

Stir 1 cup flour into butter mixture until just combined. Add 2/3 cup milk into butter-flour mixture; mix well. Continue adding 1 cup flour and 2/3 cup milk, alternating until all the flour and milk are used and batter is smooth. Pour batter into the 2 prepared pans.

Step 4

Bake in the preheated oven until a toothpick inserted in the center of each cake comes out clean, 30 to 40 minutes. Cool cakes completely before removing from pans, at least 2 hours.

Step 5

Beat confectioners' sugar, 1 cup butter, and 2 teaspoons vanilla extract together in a bowl with an electric mixer until icing is fluffy and smooth.

Step 6

Remove cakes from pans and slice round cake in half. Lay the square cake on a work surface so it resembles a diamond-shape. Lay 1 round cake half on the top left side of the 'diamond' cake. Lay the second round cake half on the top right side of the 'diamond' cake, creating a 'heart-shaped' cake on top. Spread icing over the assembled cake.

Nutrition Facts

Per Serving:

546 calories; protein 5.2g 11% DV; carbohydrates 76g 25% DV; fat 25.1g 39% DV; cholesterol 109.9mg 37% DV; sodium 334mg 13% DV.

Cream Cheese Frosting

Prep: 10 mins **Total:** 10 mins

Servings: 24

Yield: 3 cups

Ingredients

- 2 (8 ounce) packages cream cheese, softened
- ½ cup butter, softened
- 2 cups sifted confectioners' sugar
- 1 teaspoon vanilla extract

Directions

Step 1

In a medium bowl, cream together the cream cheese and butter until creamy. Mix in the vanilla, then gradually stir in the confectioners' sugar. Store in the refrigerator after use.

Nutrition Facts

Per Serving:

140 calories; protein 1.4g 3% DV; carbohydrates 10.9g 4% DV; fat 10.4g 16% DV; cholesterol 30.7mg 10% DV; sodium 82.6mg 3% DV.

Raspberry Sauce

Prep: 10 mins **Cook:** 5 mins **Total:** 15 mins

Servings: 8

Yield: 2 cups

Ingredients

- 1 pint fresh raspberries
- ¼ cup white sugar
- 2 tablespoons orange juice
- 2 tablespoons cornstarch
- 1 cup cold water

Directions

Step 1

Combine the raspberries, sugar, and orange juice in a saucepan. Whisk the cornstarch into the cold water until smooth. Add the mixture to the saucepan and bring to a boil.

Step 2

Simmer for about 5 minutes, stirring constantly, until the desired consistency is reached. The sauce will thicken further as it cools.

Step 3

Puree the sauce in a blender or with a handheld immersion blender and strain it through a fine sieve. Serve warm or cold. The sauce will keep in the refrigerator for up to two weeks.

Nutrition Facts

Per Serving:

53 calories; protein 0.4g 1% DV; carbohydrates 13g 4% DV; fat 0.2g; cholesterolmg; sodium 1.1mg.

White Chocolate Raspberry Cheesecake

Prep: 1 hr **Cook:** 1 hr **Additional:** 8 hrs **Total:** 10 hrs

Servings: 16

Yield: 1 - 9 inch cheesecake

Ingredients

- 1 cup chocolate cookie crumbs
- 3 tablespoons white sugar
- ¼ cup butter, melted
- 1 (10 ounce) package frozen raspberries
- 2 tablespoons white sugar
- 2 teaspoons cornstarch
- ½ cup water
- 2 cups white chocolate chips
- ½ cup half-and-half cream
- 3 (8 ounce) packages cream cheese, softened
- ½ cup white sugar
- 3 large eggs eggs
- 1 teaspoon vanilla extract

Directions

Step 1

In a medium bowl, mix together cookie crumbs, 3 tablespoons sugar, and melted butter. Press mixture into the bottom of a 9 inch springform pan.

Step 2

In a saucepan, combine raspberries, 2 tablespoons sugar, cornstarch, and water. Bring to boil, and continue boiling 5 minutes, or until sauce is thick. Strain sauce through a mesh strainer to remove seeds.

Step 3

Preheat oven to 325 degrees F (165 degrees C). In a metal bowl over a pan of simmering water, melt white chocolate chips with half-and-half, stirring occasionally until smooth.

Step 4

In a large bowl, mix together cream cheese and 1/2 cup sugar until smooth. Beat in eggs one at a time. Blend in vanilla and melted white chocolate. Pour half of batter over crust. Spoon 3 tablespoons raspberry sauce over batter. Pour remaining cheesecake batter into pan, and again spoon 3 tablespoons raspberry sauce over the top. Swirl batter with the tip of a knife to create a marbled effect.

Step 5

Bake for 55 to 60 minutes, or until filling is set. Cool, cover with plastic wrap, and refrigerate for 8 hours before removing from pan. Serve with remaining raspberry sauce.

Nutrition Facts

Per Serving:

412 calories; protein 6.8g 14% DV; carbohydrates 34.4g 11% DV; fat 28.3g 44% DV; cholesterol 96.4mg 32% DV; sodium 225.8mg 9% DV.

Death By Chocolate

Servings: 16

Yield: 1 - punch bowl

Ingredients

- 1 (19.8 ounce) package brownie mix
- 2 (3.9 ounce) packages instant chocolate pudding mix
- 1 (16 ounce) package frozen whipped topping, thawed
- 3 (1.4 ounce) bars chocolate covered English toffee

Directions

Step 1

Prepare brownies according to package directions. Let cool.

Step 2

Mix pudding according to package directions.

Step 3

In a glass punch bowl, layer in the following order: 1/2 of the brownie, crumbled; 1/2 of the pudding; 1 toffee bar, crushed; 1/2 of the whipped topping.

Step 4

Repeat layers in the same order. Save the last toffee bar to crumble and sprinkle on top before serving.

Step 5

Refrigerate. Best if made the day before you serve it.

Nutrition Facts

Per Serving:

330 calories; protein 2.3g 5% DV; carbohydrates 49.5g 16% DV; fat 14.9g 23% DV; cholesterol 3.9mg 1% DV; sodium 330.2mg 13% DV.

Flourless Chocolate Cake

Prep: 15 mins **Cook:** 30 mins **Additional:** 1 hr 10 mins **Total:** 1 hr 55 mins

Servings: 8

Yield: 1 8-inch single layer cake

Ingredients

- 4 (1 ounce) squares semisweet chocolate, chopped
- ½ cup butter
- ¾ cup white sugar
- ½ cup cocoa powder
- 3 large eggs eggs, beaten
- 1 teaspoon vanilla extract

Directions

Step 1

Preheat oven to 300 degrees F (150 degrees C). Grease an 8 inch round cake pan, and dust with cocoa powder.

Step 2

In the top of a double boiler over lightly simmering water, melt chocolate and butter. Remove from heat, and stir in sugar, cocoa powder, eggs, and vanilla. Pour into prepared pan.

Step 3

Bake in preheated oven for 30 minutes. Let cool in pan for 10 minutes, then turn out onto a wire rack and cool completely. Slices can also be reheated for 20 to 30 seconds in the microwave before serving.

Nutrition Facts

Per Serving:

285 calories; protein 4.5g 9% DV; carbohydrates 29.9g 10% DV; fat 18.6g 29% DV; cholesterol 100.3mg 33% DV; sodium 109.1mg 4% DV.

Cake Balls

Prep: 40 mins **Cook:** 30 mins **Additional:** 2 hrs **Total:** 3 hrs 10 mins

Servings: 36

Yield: 3 dozen

Ingredients

- 1 (18.25 ounce) package chocolate cake mix
- 1 (16 ounce) container prepared chocolate frosting
- 1 (3 ounce) bar chocolate flavored confectioners coating

Directions

Step 1

Prepare the cake mix according to package directions using any of the recommended pan sizes. When cake is done, crumble while warm into a large bowl, and stir in the frosting until well blended.

Step 2

Melt chocolate coating in a glass bowl in the microwave, or in a metal bowl over a pan of simmering water, stirring occasionally until smooth.

Step 3

Use a melon baller or small scoop to form balls of the chocolate cake mixture. Dip the balls in chocolate using a toothpick or fork to hold them. Place on waxed paper to set.

Cook's Note:

If you want to go the extra mile, cake balls can be rolled in nuts, sprinkles, coconut, etc. or double-dipped in white and dark chocolates. White chocolate confectioners' coating is also called Almond Bark in some stores.

Nutrition Facts

Per Serving:

124 calories; protein 1.1g 2% DV; carbohydrates 19.7g 6% DV; fat 5.2g 8% DV; cholesterol 0.5mg; sodium 143.4mg 6% DV.

Chocolate Lava Cake

Prep: 5 mins **Cook:** 25 mins **Additional:** 45 mins **Total:** 1 hr 15 mins

Servings: 4

Yield: 4 servings

Ingredients

- butter as needed
- 2 large egg yolks egg yolks
- 2 large eggs eggs
- 3 tablespoons white sugar
- 3 ½ ounces chopped dark chocolate
- 5 tablespoons butter
- 4 teaspoons unsweetened cocoa powder
- 3 tablespoons flour
- 1 pinch salt
- ⅛ teaspoon vanilla extract

Directions

Step 1

Generously butter the inside of 4 (5 1/2 ounce) ramekins. Place them in a casserole dish.

Step 2

Whisk together egg yolks, eggs, and sugar in a bowl until light, foamy, and lemon colored.

Step 3

Melt chocolate and butter in a microwave-safe bowl in 30-second intervals, stirring after each melting, 1 to 3 minutes.

Step 4

Stir melted chocolate mixture into egg and sugar mixture until combined.

Step 5

Sift cocoa powder into the mixture; stir to combine.

Step 6

Sift flour and salt into the mixture; stir to combine into a batter.

Step 7

Stir vanilla extract into the batter.

Step 8

Transfer batter to a resealable plastic bag. Snip one corner of the bag with scissors to create a tip.

Step 9

Divide batter evenly between the prepared ramekins; tap gently on the counter to remove any air bubbles.

Step 10

Refrigerate 30 minutes.

Step 11

Preheat an oven to 425 degrees F (220 degrees C).

Step 12

Arrange the ramekins in a casserole dish. Pour enough hot tap water into the casserole dish to reach halfway up the sides of the ramekins.

Step 13

Bake in the preheated over for 15-18 minutes. Set aside to cool for 15 minutes.

Step 14

Loosen the edges from the ramekin with a knife. Invert each cake onto a plate and dust with powdered sugar.

Nutrition Facts

Per Serving:

394 calories; protein 6.9g 14% DV; carbohydrates 32g 10% DV; fat 28.7g 44% DV; cholesterol 241.2mg 80% DV; sodium 207.4mg 8% DV.

Dobos Torte

Prep: 30 mins **Cook:** 1 hr **Additional:** 1 hr 30 mins **Total:** 3 hrs

Servings: 12

Yield: 1 9-inch 6-layer cake

Ingredients

- 9 large egg whites egg whites
- 8 large egg yolks egg yolks
- 1 cup white sugar
- ¼ cup milk
- 1 tablespoon lemon zest
- 1 pinch salt

- 1 ½ teaspoons vanilla extract
- 1 ½ cups sifted all-purpose flour
- ½ tablespoon shortening
- 1 cup white sugar
- 1 recipe Chocolate Buttercream

Directions

Step 1

Preheat oven to 400 degrees F (205 degrees C). Have ready two 10-inch cardboard circles. Generously grease a 9-inch springform pan with soft butter, and dust with flour.

Step 2

Beat the egg whites until frothy, and gradually add 1 cup sugar. Beat just to soft peaks. In another bowl, beat the yolks with the milk, lemon peel, vanilla, and salt. Fold this into the egg whites. Sift the flour over the egg mixture, and fold in.

Step 3

Spread 1 1/3 cups batter into the prepared pan. Bake for about 5 to 9 minutes, or until small, brown spots begin to appear on cake. Remove the cake from the oven, and remove layer from pan with a spatula. Dust the cake lightly with flour, and place on a rack to cool. Grease pan again, and repeat this process until all of the batter is used, about 6 times more. Place the layers between wax paper, and cover with a towel. Chill layers for a few hours. Make the Chocolate Buttercream.

Step 4

Layer the chilled layers on one of the cardboard rounds with the buttercream. Start with one layer; cover with the buttercream, and then press down with another layer to make a good seal. Repeat this with the remaining layers, but reserve one layer. Wrap the cake in plastic, and chill for at least 6 hours along with the remaining buttercream. Grease the other cardboard round with the shortening, and place the last layer on it.

Step 5

Place 1 cup sugar into a non-stick skillet over medium heat. Allow sugar to cook until the edges look melted and brown. Begin stirring with a wooden spoon. Cook until the sugar become an amber color, and is smooth. Carefully pour the caramel over the top of the last layer, and spread to the edges with an oiled knife. Quickly, using an oiled knife, indent the top of the caramel into 16 wedges. Allow to cool slightly, and then retouch the indents with the knife again. Place layer onto a counter top dusted with sugar, and allow the caramel to cool completely.

Step 6

Place some more buttercream on top of the chilled torte, and top with the caramel round. Frost the sides with the remaining buttercream. Chill the torte before serving.

Nutrition Facts

Per Serving:

242 calories; protein 6.3g 13% DV; carbohydrates 46.2g 15% DV; fat 3.7g 6% DV; cholesterol 137mg 46% DV; sodium 49.4mg 2% DV.

Strawberry Crepe Cake

Prep: 30 mins **Cook:** 1 hr **Additional:** 45 mins **Total:** 2 hrs 15 mins

Servings: 12

Yield: 1 20-layer crepe cake

Ingredients

For the Crepes:

- 5 large eggs
- 2 ½ cups all-purpose flour
- 2 tablespoons white sugar
- ½ teaspoon kosher salt
- 2 ½ tablespoons vegetable oil
- 3 ¼ cups whole milk
- ½ teaspoon vanilla extract
- 4 tablespoons butter, or as needed

For the Fruit Mixture:

- 1 (10 ounce) jar strawberry jam
- 2 tablespoons water

For the Cream Filling:

- ¾ cup mascarpone cheese
- 1 ½ cups heavy cream
- 3 tablespoons white sugar
- ½ teaspoon vanilla extract

Directions

Step 1

Pour eggs, flour, sugar, salt, oil, milk, and vanilla extract into a blender. Blend, starting on low speed and finishing on high, until combined. Refrigerate batter for at least 30 minutes.

Step 2

Scoop strawberry jam into a saucepan. Rinse out jar with water and pour into the saucepan. Bring to a simmer over medium heat and stir. Simmer for 1 minute, remove from heat, and stir. Let cool to room temperature.

Step 3

Brush some butter over a nonstick skillet over medium heat. Pour in 1/4 cup batter; tilt pan to coat evenly. Cook until crepes bubble and brown, about 1 1/2 minutes per side. Transfer to a baking sheet. Repeat with remaining batter, buttering the pan between crepes. Let cool completely before stacking, at least 15 minutes.

Step 4

Combine mascarpone cheese, cream, sugar, and vanilla extract in a bowl. Whisk together until stiff peaks form.

Step 5

Lay a crepe onto a large plate. Spoon on 2 or 3 tablespoons of the cream mixture, spreading it almost to the edge. Swirl in some strawberry jam. Transfer finished crepe onto a flat serving plate. Repeat with remaining crepes, cream, and jam. Center each crepe over the previous one in a stack. Gently press on a final plain crepe to finish.

Step 6

Refrigerate until completely chilled before cutting and serving.

Notes:

I was going for a very light dessert here, in both taste and texture, but this technique really shines if you use a more traditional cake filling like buttercream. Since that gets nice and firm when chilled, you'll get even more gorgeously defined layers.

I probably could've just folded the strawberry jam into the whipped cream mixture to save time when assembling. I thought it would be nice to have streaks of fruit in the cream, but once sliced, it really wasn't that noticeable. Of course fresh fruit would also work, just be aware of the extra moisture that might add.

Nutrition Facts

Per Serving:

466 calories; protein 9.1g 18% DV; carbohydrates 44.5g 14% DV; fat 28.7g 44% DV; cholesterol 152.5mg 51% DV; sodium 182.3mg 7% DV.

German Marble Cake

Servings: 14

Yield: 1 -10 inch tube cake

Ingredients

- 1 cup butter
- 1 ½ cups white sugar
- 4 large eggs eggs
- 1 cup milk
- 1 teaspoon almond extract
- 3 ¼ cups all-purpose flour
- 1 tablespoon baking powder
- ⅛ teaspoon salt
- ¼ cup unsweetened cocoa powder
- 3 tablespoons dark rum

Directions

Step 1

Preheat oven to 350 degrees F (175 degrees C). Grease and flour one 10 inch tube pan.

Step 2

In a large bowl, cream the butter with the sugar. Beat in the eggs, then the milk and almond extract.

Step 3

In another bowl, stir together the flour, baking powder and salt. Beat the flour mixture into the creamed mixture. Turn half of the batter into another bowl and stir in the cocoa and rum.

Step 4

Layer the light and dark batters by large spoonfuls and then swirl slightly with a knife.

Step 5

Bake the cake in at 350 degree F (175 degree C) for about 70 minutes, or until it tests done with a toothpick. Transfer to a rack to cool. Makes about 14 to 16 servings.

Nutrition Facts

Per Serving:

346 calories; protein 5.8g 12% DV; carbohydrates 45.6g 15% DV; fat 15.4g 24% DV; cholesterol 89.4mg 30% DV; sodium 246.7mg 10% DV.

Italian Love Cake

Prep: 25 mins **Cook:** 1 hr 30 mins **Additional:** 1 hr **Total:** 2 hrs 55 mins

Servings: 18

Yield: 1 - 9 x 13 inch cake

Ingredients

- 1 (18.25 ounce) package chocolate cake mix
- 2 pints part-skim ricotta cheese
- ¾ cup white sugar
- 1 teaspoon vanilla extract
- 4 large eggs eggs
- 1 (3.9 ounce) package instant chocolate pudding mix
- 1 cup milk
- 1 (12 ounce) container frozen whipped topping, thawed

Directions

Step 1

Prepare cake mix as directed on box. Pour batter into 9 x 13 x 2 inch greased baking dish. Set aside.

Step 2

Combine ricotta cheese, sugar, vanilla, and eggs. Blend well. Spread mixture evenly over the top of the cake batter.

Step 3

Bake at 350 degrees F (175 degrees C) for 75 minutes if using a glass baking dish, 90 minutes if using a metal pan.

Step 4

Blend pudding mix and milk until thickened. Blend in whipped topping. Spread over cooled cake.

Nutrition Facts

Per Serving:

348 calories; protein 11.1g 22% DV; carbohydrates 42.9g 14% DV; fat 15.7g 24% DV; cholesterol 62mg 21% DV; sodium 428.4mg 17% DV.

Fresh Strawberry Upside Down Cake

Prep: 15 mins **Cook:** 50 mins **Additional:** 15 mins **Total:** 1 hr 20 mins

Servings: 12

Yield: 12 servings

Ingredients

- 2 cups crushed fresh strawberries
- 1 (6 ounce) package strawberry flavored Jell-O mix
- 3 cups miniature marshmallows
- 1 (18 ounce) package yellow cake mix, batter prepared as directed on package

Directions

Step 1

Preheat an oven to 350 degrees F (175 degrees C).

Step 2

Spread crushed strawberries on the bottom of a 9x13 inch baking pan. Evenly sprinkle strawberries with the dry gelatin powder, and top with mini marshmallows.

Step 3

Prepare the cake mix as directed on the package, and pour on top of the marshmallows. Bake in the preheated oven until a toothpick inserted into the center comes out clean, about 40 to 50 minutes. Cool in the pan for 15 minutes. Run a knife around the pan to loosen the sides, and turn the cake out onto a serving tray. Store cake in the refrigerator.

Nutrition Facts

Per Serving:

290 calories; protein 3.1g 6% DV; carbohydrates 58.3g 19% DV; fat 5g 8% DV; cholesterol 0.8mg; sodium 330.7mg 13% DV.

Eclair Cake with Chocolate Ganache

Prep: 30 mins **Cook:** 25 mins **Additional:** 1 hr 45 mins **Total:** 2 hrs 40 mins

Servings: 12

Yield: 1 9 x 13-inch dish

Ingredients

Pastry Shell:

- 1 cup water
- ½ cup butter
- ¼ teaspoon salt

- 1 cup all-purpose flour
- 4 eaches eggs

Filling:

- 2 cups cold heavy whipping cream
- 2 tablespoons confectioners' sugar
- 1 teaspoon vanilla extract
- 2 (3.5 ounce) packages instant vanilla pudding mix

- 2 cups cold milk
- Chocolate Ganache:
- 1 cup bittersweet chocolate, chopped
- 1 cup heavy cream

Directions

Step 1

Preheat an oven to 400 degrees F (200 degrees C). Grease a 9x13-inch baking dish. Place a mixing bowl in the freezer to chill.

Step 2

Combine the water, butter, and salt in a medium saucepan and bring to a boil over medium-high heat. Reduce the heat to medium and stir in the flour. Cook and stir until the mixture pulls away from the sides of the pan and forms a ball. Transfer the mixture to a mixing bowl and beat in the eggs, one at a time, until fully incorporated. Spread the dough evenly in the bottom of the baking dish.

Step 3

Bake the pastry in the preheated oven until golden brown, 25 to 30 minutes. (The dough will rise and make a boat shape, but should drop as it cools.) Cool completely on wire rack.

Step 4

Remove the chilled mixing bowl from the freezer and pour in 2 cups of cold whipping cream. Whip until the cream thickens, about 1 minute; stir in the confectioners' sugar and the vanilla extract. Continue to whip until the cream forms stiff peaks. Refrigerate the whipped cream while you mix the pudding.

Step 5

Pour the pudding mixes and the milk into a mixing bowl and stir until creamy. Fold in the whipped cream. Spread the filling over the cooled crust and refrigerate.

Step 6

Place the chopped chocolate in a heat-proof bowl. Bring 1 cup of cream almost to a boil in a small saucepan over medium heat. Pour the hot cream over the chocolate and allow it to soften for 1 minute. Whisk the mixture until smooth. Let the mixture cool slightly to thicken, about 10 minutes. Pour the ganache over the cream filling, spreading to cover the entire surface. Return the pan to the refrigerator and chill for at least 1 hour before serving.

Nutrition Facts

Per Serving:

530 calories; protein 6.9g 14% DV; carbohydrates 39.6g 13% DV; fat 38.9g 60% DV; cholesterol 160.5mg 54% DV; sodium 400mg 16% DV.

Boscobel Beach Ginger Cake

Prep: 30 mins **Cook:** 45 mins **Total:** 1 hr 15 mins

Servings: 12

Yield: 1 - 9 inch Bundt pan

Ingredients

- 1 cup butter
- 1 ¼ cups packed brown sugar
- 4 large eggs eggs
- ¼ cup grated fresh ginger root
- 1 teaspoon vanilla extract
- 1 cup milk
- 2 ½ cups all-purpose flour
- 4 teaspoons baking powder
- 4 teaspoons ground ginger
- 1 ½ teaspoons ground cinnamon
- ½ teaspoon salt
- 2 tablespoons confectioners' sugar for dusting

Directions

Step 1

Preheat oven to 350 degrees F (175 degrees C). Grease and flour a 9 inch Bundt pan. Sift together the flour, baking powder, ground ginger, cinnamon and salt. Set aside.

Step 2

In a large bowl, cream together the butter and brown sugar until light and fluffy. Beat in the eggs one at a time, then stir in the grated ginger root and vanilla. Beat in the flour mixture alternately with the milk, mixing just until incorporated. Pour batter into prepared pan.

Step 3

Bake in the preheated oven for 45 to 50 minutes, or until a toothpick inserted into the center of the cake comes out clean. Let cool in pan for 10 minutes, then turn out onto a serving plate. Dust lightly with confectioners' sugar before serving.

Nutrition Facts

Per Serving:

362 calories; protein 5.7g 12% DV; carbohydrates 46g 15% DV; fat 17.7g 27% DV; cholesterol 104.3mg 35% DV; sodium 364.9mg 15% DV.

Heavenly Chipped Chocolate and Hazelnut Cheesecake

Prep: 1 hr **Cook:** 1 hr **Additional:** 1 hr **Total:** 3 hrs

Servings: 12

Yield: 1 9-inch cheesecake

Ingredients

- ⅓ cup semisweet chocolate chips
- 1 ½ cups vanilla wafer crumbs
- ¾ cup hazelnuts - toasted, skinned and coarsely chopped
- 2 tablespoons white sugar
- 3 tablespoons butter, melted
- 3 (8 ounce) packages cream cheese, softened
- 1 cup white sugar
- 3 large eggs eggs, lightly beaten
- 3 tablespoons hazelnut liqueur
- 1 cup semisweet chocolate chips
- ⅔ cup semisweet chocolate chips
- 13 nuts skinned, toasted hazelnuts
- ¼ cup sour cream, room temperature
- 1 tablespoon hazelnut liqueur

Directions

Step 1

Preheat oven to 300 degrees F (150 degrees C).

Step 2

Using a blender or a food processor, finely chop 1/3 cup semisweet chocolate chips. Transfer ground chocolate to a mixing bowl. Add vanilla wafer crumbs, ground hazelnuts, 2 tablespoons white sugar, and melted butter or margarine. Mix until well combined. Press onto the bottom and up the sides of a 9 inch springform pan. Bake in preheated oven for 15 minutes. Allow to cool.

Step 3

Raise oven temperature to 350 degrees F (175 degrees C).

Step 4

In a large bowl, beat the cream cheese until fluffy. Gradually add 1 cup white sugar; mix well. Add the eggs and 3 tablespoons liqueur. Mix until well blended. Coarsely chop 1 cup of the semisweet chocolate chips, and stir the chocolate into the cream cheese mixture. Pour batter into the cooled crust.

Step 5

Bake in preheated 350 degrees F (175 degrees C) oven for 1 hour. Let cake cool in oven for 1 hour. Remove outer ring from pan; allow cake to cool completely.

Step 6

Melt 2/3 cup semisweet chocolate chips over hot (not boiling) water. Stir until smooth. Dip 13 hazelnuts into the chocolate, covering one-half of each nut. Shake off the excess chocolate. Place on a waxed-paper lined plate and chill until set.

Step 7

Stir the sour cream into the remaining melted chocolate and mix well. Add 1 tablespoon liqueur. Spread glaze on top of the cooled cheesecake. Garnish with chocolate-dipped hazelnuts.

Nutrition Facts

Per Serving:

638 calories; protein 9.5g 19% DV; carbohydrates 58g 19% DV; fat 43g 66% DV; cholesterol 117.8mg 39% DV; sodium 278.5mg 11% DV.

Chocolate Decadence

Prep: 15 mins **Cook:** 15 mins **Additional:** 1 hr 30 mins **Total:** 2 hrs

Servings: 12

Yield: 1 9-inch cake

Ingredients

- 18 ounces semisweet chocolate, chopped
- 10 tablespoons unsalted butter
- 5 large eggs large eggs, at room temperature
- 4 teaspoons white sugar
- 4 teaspoons all-purpose flour
- 1 pinch cayenne pepper
- 1 pinch salt

Directions

Step 1

Preheat oven to 425 degrees F (220 degrees C). Butter and flour a 9-inch cake pan.

Step 2

Melt semisweet chocolate and unsalted butter together in the top of a double boiler over simmering water, stirring frequently and scraping down the sides with a rubber spatula, until chocolate and butter are completely melted and combined. Remove from heat.

Step 3

Beat eggs and sugar together in a bowl with a whisk or an electric mixer until pale and very thick, 5 to 10 minutes. Sift in flour, cayenne, and salt; whisk to combine.

Step 4

Pour 1/4 of the egg mixture into chocolate mixture; stir to combine. Pour chocolate mixture into remaining egg mixture and stir until cake batter is combined. Pour batter into prepared cake pan.

Step 5

Bake in the preheated oven until just barely set, with a jiggle below the surface, 14 to 15 minutes. Cool to room temperature, wrap in aluminum foil, and refrigerate until chilled, at least 1 hour.

Cook's Note:

If you want to remove your cake from the pan for presentation, just set it in a pan of hot water for a minute and it will pop right out.

Per Serving:

333 calories; protein 5.8g 12% DV; carbohydrates 26.2g 9% DV; fat 25.2g 39% DV; cholesterol 102.9mg 34% DV; sodium 43.4mg 2% DV.

Cassata Cake

Servings: 12

Yield: 1 -9 Inch cake

Ingredients

- 1 ½ cups cake flour
- ½ teaspoon baking powder
- ¼ teaspoon salt
- 5 large eggs eggs
- ½ cup cold water
- 1 ¼ cups white sugar
- 1 teaspoon vanilla extract
- ½ teaspoon cream of tartar
- 2 pounds whole milk ricotta cheese
- 2 ¼ cups confectioners' sugar
- ½ teaspoon ground cinnamon
- 1 ½ teaspoons vanilla extract
- 2 (1 ounce) squares semi-sweet chocolate
- ½ cup candied lemon peel
- ⅓ cup white sugar
- ¼ cup water
- 2 tablespoons light rum
- 6 (1 ounce) squares bittersweet chocolate, chopped
- ⅓ cup heavy whipping cream
- 3 tablespoons unsalted butter, cubed

Directions

Step 1

Preheat the oven to 325 degrees F (165 degrees C). Grease and line with parchment paper 2 nine inch round layer pans.

Step 2

Sift the flour, baking powder, and salt together.

Step 3

Separate the eggs and set the egg whites aside. Beat the egg yolks together on medium-high speed until very thick, about 4 minutes. Gradually add the cold water. Add 1- 1/4 cups of the white sugar, slowly, and beat well for about 3 more minutes. Add 1 teaspoon of the vanilla. Sift the flour mixture over the egg yolk mixture and fold in.

Step 4

Beat the egg whites and cream of tartar together until stiff peaks form. Fold this into the yolk mixture. Divide batter between the pans.

Step 5

Bake at 325 degrees F (165 degrees C) for 25 minutes. Cool on rack for 10 minutes and then invert and cool completely.

Step 6

Cut each cake layer in half. Place one of the 4 halves on a cake board or plate and sprinkle with a little of the Rum Syrup. Spread about 1-1/2 cups of the Filling over this layer. Add a second layer of cake and repeat this procedure. Top the cake with the last layer of cake. Chill at least 4 hours. Spread Chocolate Glaze over top of cake.

Step 7

To Make Ricotta Cheese Filling: Beat the ricotta cheese well and add the confectioner's sugar and cinnamon. Add 1-1/2 teaspoons of the vanilla and grate 2 ounces of the chocolate in using the coarse side of a grater. Stir in the candied lemon peel and mix. Chill until ready to use.

Step 8

To Make The Rum Syrup: Place 1/3 cup of the sugar and the water in a small saucepan. Bring to a boil over medium heat, stirring to dissolve sugar. Boil 1 minute and then remove from heat and add the rum. Cool to room temperature.

Step 9

To Make The Chocolate Glaze: Melt 6 ounces of the chocolate and the cream in the microwave, whisk smooth. Add the butter and whisk until dissolved. Cool mixture until spreadable. Spread over the top of the cake.

Nutrition Facts

Per Serving:

601 calories; protein 14.1g 28% DV; carbohydrates 84.1g 27% DV; fat 23.6g 36% DV; cholesterol 133.4mg 45% DV; sodium 174.2mg 7% DV.

French Chocolate Cake

Prep: 35 mins **Cook:** 45 mins **Additional:** 1 hr **Total:** 2 hrs 20 mins

Servings: 12

Yield: 1 9-inch cake

Ingredients

- ½ cup white sugar
- 10 (1 ounce) squares semi-sweet chocolate
- ¾ cup unsalted butter, cubed
- 2 teaspoons vanilla extract
- 5 large eggs eggs, separated
- ¼ cup sifted all-purpose flour
- 1 dash cream of tartar
- salt to taste
- ½ tablespoon confectioners' sugar, for dusting

Directions

Step 1

Preheat the oven to 325 degrees F (165 degrees C). Generously grease a 9-inch springform cake tin. Dust with a little sugar, and tap out the excess.

Step 2

Set aside 3 tablespoons of the sugar. Place the chocolate, butter, and remaining sugar in a large, heavy-based pan. Cook over moderate heat until the chocolate and butter have melted, and the sugar has dissolved. Remove the pan from heat. Stir in the vanilla, and leave the mixture to cool slightly.

Step 3

Beat the egg yolks into the chocolate mixture one at a time, beating well after each addition. Stir in the flour.

Step 4

In a large bowl, scrupulously clean and grease-free, beat the egg whites until foamy. Add the cream of tartar and salt, and beat to stiff peaks. Sprinkle reserved sugar over egg whites, and beat until stiff and glossy. Use a whisk or spatula to fold 1/3 of the egg whites into the chocolate mixture, then carefully fold in the remaining whites. Carefully pour batter into the prepared tin, and tap the tin gently to release air bubbles.

Step 5

Bake until well risen and a skewer inserted into the center of the cake comes out clean, for about 45 minutes to 1 hour. Check the cake after 30 minutes: if the cake appears to rise unevenly, rotate after 30 to 35 minutes. If the cake starts to crack or become too brown, place a piece of foil lightly over the top. Transfer the cake to a wire cooling rack, and remove the sides of the springform tin. Cool completely, and then remove the base. Do not attempt to remove the cake before it's completely cooled as this cake is very fragile.

Nutrition Facts

Per Serving:

294 calories; protein 4.7g 9% DV; carbohydrates 24.3g 8% DV; fat 21.1g 33% DV; cholesterol 108mg 36% DV; sodium 30.9mg 1% DV.

Black Forest Cake

Prep: 30 mins **Cook:** 40 mins **Additional:** 1 hr **Total:** 2 hrs 10 mins

Servings: 12

Yield: 2 layer 8 inch round cake

Ingredients

- 1 ⅔ cups all-purpose flour
- ⅔ cup unsweetened cocoa powder
- 1 ½ teaspoons baking soda
- 1 teaspoon salt
- ½ cup shortening
- 1 ½ cups white sugar
- 2 large eggs eggs
- 1 teaspoon vanilla extract
- 1 ½ cups buttermilk
- ½ cup kirschwasser
- ½ cup butter
- 3 ½ cups confectioners' sugar
- 1 pinch salt
- 1 teaspoon strong brewed coffee
- 2 (14 ounce) cans pitted Bing cherries, drained
- 2 cups heavy whipping cream
- ½ teaspoon vanilla extract
- 1 tablespoon kirschwasser
- 1 (1 ounce) square semisweet chocolate

Directions

Step 1

Preheat oven to 350 degrees F (175 degrees C). Line the bottoms of two 8 inch round pans with parchment paper circles. Sift together flour, cocoa, baking soda and 1 teaspoon salt. Set aside.

Step 2

Cream shortening and sugar until light and fluffy. Beat in eggs and vanilla. Beat in flour mixture, alternating with buttermilk, until combined. Pour into 2 round 8 inch pans.

Step 3

Bake at 350 degrees F (175 degrees C) for 35 to 40 minutes, or until a toothpick inserted into the cake comes out clean. Cool completely. Remove paper from the cakes. Cut each layer in half, horizontally, making 4 layers total. Sprinkle layers with the 1/2 cup kirshwasser.

Step 4

In a medium bowl, cream the butter until light and fluffy. Add confectioners sugar, pinch of salt, and coffee; beat until smooth. If the consistency is too thick, add a couple teaspoons of cherry juice or milk. Spread first layer of cake with 1/3 of the filling. Top with 1/3 of the cherries. Repeat with the remaining layers.

Step 5

In a separate bowl, whip the cream to stiff peaks. Beat in 1/2 teaspoon vanilla and 1 tablespoon kirshwasser. Frost top and sides of cake. Sprinkle with chocolate curls made by using a potato peeler on semisweet baking chocolate.

Nutrition Facts

Per Serving:

693 calories; protein 6.4g 13% DV; carbohydrates 88.8g 29% DV; fat 33.6g 52% DV; cholesterol 106.9mg 36% DV; sodium 468.3mg 19% DV.

Best Ever Strawberry Cake

Prep: 40 mins **Cook:** 25 mins **Additional:** 10 mins **Total:** 1 hr 15 mins

Servings: 12

Yield: 12 servings

Ingredients

- 1 cup pureed strawberries
- ¼ cup 2% milk
- 6 large eggs eggs
- 1 tablespoon vanilla extract
- 2 ¼ cups sifted cake flour
- 1 ¾ cups white sugar
- 4 teaspoons baking powder
- 1 teaspoon salt
- ¾ cup butter, softened

- 2 (8 ounce) packages cream cheese, softened
- ½ cup butter, softened
- 2 cups confectioners' sugar
- 1 teaspoon vanilla extract

Directions

Step 1

Preheat oven to 350 degrees F (175 degrees C).

Step 2

Grease and flour two 8-inch cake pans.

Step 3

Mix pureed strawberries, milk, eggs, and 1 tablespoon vanilla extract together in a small bowl; transfer to the bowl of a stand mixer.

Step 4

Beat flour, white sugar, baking powder, and salt into strawberry mixture on Low; add butter and continue beating on Low until evenly combined.

Step 5

Stop mixer, scrape sides, and beat again for about 30 seconds.

Step 6

Divide batter evenly between the two prepared cake pans.

Step 7

Bake in the preheated oven until a toothpick inserted into the center of each cake comes out clean, about 25 minutes. Cool the cakes in the pans for about 10 minutes; transfer to wire racks to completely cool, about 30 minutes.

Step 8

Beat cream cheese and butter together in a medium bowl until smooth. Gradually beat confectioners' sugar into cream cheese mixture until creamy and fluffy; stir in 1 teaspoon vanilla extract.

Step 9

Spread about 1/2 the frosting on top of 1 cake. Place second cake on top of frosting layer; spread the remaining frosting on top of second cake and around sides of both cakes.

Cook's Notes:

To make strawberry puree, put frozen or fresh strawberries into a blender or food processor and puree.

Be sure to use softened butter, NOT melted. Unsalted or salted butter will work. When using salted butter, simply reduce the salt in recipe to 1/2 teaspoon. Also, all-purpose flour works in this recipe, but cake flour is recommended.

For sheet cake: Grease and flour one 9x13 pan. Bake for 20 minutes and insert a toothpick in the center of the cake. If it doesn't come out clean, continue baking in increments of 2 to 3 minutes until the toothpick comes out clean. Allow to cool for 10 minutes in the pan and then transfer to a wire rack to completely cool.

Optional: add 1/2 cup strawberry puree to frosting for extra strawberry flavor.

Nutrition Facts

Per Serving:

641 calories; protein 8.7g 17% DV; carbohydrates 74.5g 24% DV; fat 35.1g 54% DV; cholesterol 185.3mg 62% DV; sodium 641.2mg 26% DV.

Cherry Chocolate Cake

Servings: 24

Yield: 1 -9x13 inch cake

Ingredients

- ½ cup butter
- 1 ½ cups white sugar
- 2 large eggs eggs
- 1 teaspoon almond extract
- ½ cup unsweetened cocoa powder
- 1 ¾ cups cake flour
- 1 ¼ teaspoons baking soda
- 1 teaspoon salt
- 1 (21 ounce) can cherry pie filling

Directions

Step 1

Preheat oven to 350 degrees F (175 degrees C). Lightly grease and flour one 9x13 inch baking pan.

Step 2

Cream the butter with sugar until light and fluffy. Mix in the eggs and almond extract and beat well. Add the cocoa powder and mix until well combined.

Step 3

By hand, stir the cake flour, baking soda and salt together. Add flour mixture to the butter mixture and mix until just combined. Stir in the cherry pie filling. Pour the batter into the prepared pan.

Step 4

Bake at 350 degrees F (175 degrees C) for 30 to 35 minutes or until a toothpick inserted near the middle comes out clean. Cool and frost with Chocolate Buttercream.

Nutrition Facts

Per Serving:

159 calories; protein 1.9g 4% DV; carbohydrates 28.6g 9% DV; fat 4.6g 7% DV; cholesterol 25.7mg 9% DV; sodium 200.6mg 8% DV.

White Chocolate Cheesecake with White Chocolate Brandy Sauce

Prep: 30 mins **Cook:** 1 hr **Additional:** 9 hrs **Total:** 10 hrs 30 mins

Servings: 12

Yield: 1 10-inch cheesecake

Ingredients

White Chocolate Cheesecake:

- 4 (1 ounce) squares white chocolate
- 3 (8 ounce) packages cream cheese, room temperature
- ¾ cup white sugar
- ¼ cup all-purpose flour
- 3 large eggs eggs, room temperature
- ½ cup heavy cream, room temperature
- ½ teaspoon vanilla extract

White Chocolate Brandy Sauce:

- 2 cups finely chopped white chocolate
- 1 cup heavy cream
- 2 fluid ounces brandy

Directions

Step 1

Preheat oven to 300 degrees F (150 degrees C). Wrap the outside of a 10-inch springform pan with foil. Grease the inside of the pan.

Step 2

Place the cream cheese, sugar, and flour in a mixing bowl and cream until light and fluffy. Beat in eggs one at a time, mixing well after each addition. Scrape bowl.

Step 3

Melt 4 ounces of the white chocolate. With an electric mixer on low speed, mix melted white chocolate into cream cheese mixture. Keeping electric mixer on low, slowly beat in the vanilla and 1/2 cup of heavy cream. Blend well. Pour mixture into the prepared springform pan.

Step 4

Place cheesecake pan in a water bath filled with warm water. Bake at 300 degrees F (150 degrees C) for 50 to 60 minutes, or until center of the cheesecake is just firm. Cool at room temperature for 1 hour. Refrigerate until set before removing from pan.

Step 5

To make White Chocolate Brandy Sauce: place chopped white chocolate in a heat-proof bowl. Pour 1 cup cream into a saucepan and bring it to a boil over medium-high heat. Watch carefully so it doesn't boil over. Pour hot cream over chopped white chocolate; let soften for 2 minutes. Stir with a wooden spoon until melted. Add brandy and continue stirring until incorporated. Pour over chilled cheesecake and serve.

Nutrition Facts

Per Serving:

596 calories; protein 8.9g 18% DV; carbohydrates 39.8g 13% DV; fat 44.2g 68% DV; cholesterol 157mg 52% DV; sodium 229.4mg 9% DV.

Chocolate Strawberry Shortcake

Servings: 10

Yield: 1 9-inch layer cake

Ingredients

- 2 cups all-purpose flour
- ⅓ cup white sugar
- ¼ cup cocoa powder
- 1 tablespoon baking powder
- 1 teaspoon baking soda
- ½ teaspoon salt
- ½ cup butter
- 1 cup milk
- 2 pints strawberries, sliced
- ¼ cup white sugar
- 1 (12 ounce) container frozen whipped topping, thawed
- 2 tablespoons chocolate syrup

Directions

Step 1

Preheat an oven to 400 degrees F (200 degrees C). Grease two 9 inch layer pans.

Step 2

In a large mixing bowl, combine flour, 1/3 cup sugar, cocoa, baking powder, baking soda, and salt. Cut in butter or margarine until the mixture resembles coarse crumbs. Add milk, mixing until just moistened. Spread batter evenly into two prepared layer pans.

Step 3

Bake at 400 degrees F (200 degrees C) for 15 minutes, or until a toothpick inserted in the center comes out clean. Cool.

Step 4

In a medium-size mixing bowl, combine strawberries and 1/4 cup sugar. Let the mixture stand 10 minutes.

Step 5

Cover the bottom shortcake layer with half of strawberry mixture and half of the whipped topping. Top with second shortcake layer, remaining strawberry mixture and whipped topping. Drizzle with chocolate topping.

Nutrition Facts

Per Serving:

375 calories; protein 4.9g 10% DV; carbohydrates 49.1g 16% DV; fat 19g 29% DV; cholesterol 26.4mg 9% DV; sodium 476.5mg 19% DV.

Famous Tiramisu

Prep: 45 mins **Cook:** 20 mins **Additional:** 3 hrs 55 mins **Total:** 5 hrs

Servings: 12

Yield: 1 - 9-inch round

Ingredients

LADYFINGERS

- 5 large eggs eggs, separated
- ¾ cup white sugar, divided
- 1 cup all-purpose flour
- 1 teaspoon vanilla extract
- ¾ cup confectioners' sugar for dusting

SYRUP

- 1 cup white sugar
- 1 cup boiling water
- ½ cup strong brewed coffee
- ¼ cup rum

FILLING

- 1 (8 ounce) container mascarpone cheese
- 2 cups confectioners' sugar
- ¼ cup dark rum
- 1 teaspoon vanilla extract
- 2 cups heavy cream

TOPPING

- 2 (1 ounce) squares semisweet chocolate, grated
- ⅛ cup confectioners' sugar for dusting

Directions

Step 1

Preheat oven to 350 degrees F (175 degrees C). Line baking sheets with parchment paper.

Step 2

In a medium bowl, whip egg yolks and 1/4 cup of sugar with an electric mixer until thick and pale. In a separate bowl, whip egg whites (with clean beaters) to soft peaks. Gradually sprinkle in the remaining 1/2 cup sugar while whipping to medium stiff peaks. Fold the egg yolk mixture into the egg whites. Gently fold in the flour and 1 teaspoon vanilla. The batter should be thick and pale yellow.

Step 3

Trace two 9 inch circles onto the parchment paper using a cake pan as a guide. Spread or pipe batter to completely fill inside the lines of the circles. Batter should be about 1/2 inch tall.

Step 4

Load the remaining batter into a pastry bag fitted with a half inch tip or hole. Draw parallel lines onto another piece of parchment that are 3 inches apart. Pipe the batter back and forth just between the lines in a compressed S motion, until you run out of batter. This is the part that wraps around the outside of the cake. (It helps to have it in one piece, but you can pipe individual fingers using the guidelines drawn on the paper, if you prefer.) There may be extra.

Step 5

Bake in preheated oven 10 to 15 minutes, until firm but not browned. Remove from the oven and dust generously with confectioners' sugar. Set aside to cool.

Step 6

To make the syrup, stir together 1 cup sugar, boiling water, coffee and 1/4 cup rum until sugar is dissolved. Set aside.

Step 7

To make the filling, combine mascarpone, 2 cups confectioners' sugar, dark rum and 1 teaspoon vanilla in a large bowl. Whisk together until completely smooth, scraping the bottom of the bowl to remove any lumps. Gradually whisk in the heavy cream. Whip with an electric mixer until soft peaks form. Stop whipping when the mixture shows the first sign of graininess.

Step 8

To assemble, line the sides of a 9-inch springform pan with parchment or waxed paper. Place one of the ladyfinger rounds in the bottom of the pan. Brush generously, but do not soak completely, with syrup. Place the 3-inch high ladyfinger strips around the inside edge of the pan, so that the sides are completely covered. Brush generously with syrup.

Step 9

Spread half of the filling mixture over the first ladyfinger round in the pan. Place the remaining ladyfinger round on top of the filling. Soak the second ladyfinger round with syrup until it cannot take any more. Spread the remaining filling over that and smooth the top. Sprinkle with grated chocolate. Refrigerate at least 4 hours.

Step 10

To serve, remove the sides of the pan and carefully remove the parchment or waxed paper from the outside of the cake. Dust with confectioners' sugar just before serving.

Nutrition Facts

Per Serving:

558 calories; protein 6.2g 12% DV; carbohydrates 70.2g 23% DV; fat 27g 42% DV; cholesterol 155.2mg 52% DV; sodium 55.7mg 2% DV.

BaumKuchen

Prep: 30 mins **Cook:** 40 mins **Additional:** 20 mins **Total:** 1 hr 30 mins

Servings: 12

Yield: 1 -9 inch square cake

Ingredients

- ⅞ cup unsalted butter, softened
- 1 cup sifted confectioners' sugar
- ⅞ cup cornstarch
- 5 ½ ounces almond paste
- 1 ½ teaspoons vanilla extract
- 1 pinch salt
- 2 large egg yolks egg yolks
- 6 large egg whites egg whites
- ¾ cup white sugar
- ¾ cup all-purpose flour
- 9 (1 ounce) squares semisweet chocolate
- 2 ½ teaspoons vegetable oil

Directions

Step 1

Butter a 9 inch square metal pan. Place a sheet of parchment paper in the bottom. Butter the parchment, and flour the whole pan. Position the rack of the oven to the lowest level, and preheat the broiler.

Step 2

In a large bowl, cream the butter or margarine until light and fluffy. Add in the almond paste in small chunks; beat until smooth. Add the confectioners' sugar, cornstarch, vanilla, and salt. Beat in the yolks one at a time, beating well after each addition. Beat until smooth.

Step 3

In another bowl, beat the egg whites to soft peaks. Add in the sugar slowly while continuing to beat the meringue to stiff, glossy peaks. Fold the meringue into the yolk mixture. Sift the flour over this, and fold in.

Step 4

Spoon a small amount of batter onto the parchment in the baking pan. With a pastry brush, paint the batter on. You want to cover the paper completely, but have a thin layer. Place under the broiler, and cook until light brown; this should take about 1 to 2 minutes. Brush another layer of the batter over the cake, and place under the broiler. Continue on in this way until all of the batter is used. Cool completely. Turn the cake out of the pan, and trim the edges clean.

Step 5

In a double boiler, combine the chocolate and the oil. Heat until the chocolate is smooth. With a pastry brush, brush one side of the trimmed cake with some chocolate. Don't make it too thick. Allow this to harden. Turn the cake over, and brush the other side. Allow the cake to set. Cut the cake into 6 narrow strips, each about 1-1/2 inches wide. Brush the sides and top with the glaze, and allow to set. Store in the refrigerator, but serve at room temperature.

Nutrition Facts

Per Serving:

462 calories; protein 5.9g 12% DV; carbohydrates 55.9g 18% DV; fat 25.6g 39% DV; cholesterol 69.7mg 23% DV; sodium 32.6mg 1% DV.

Ravishing Red Velvet Cake

Prep: 30 mins **Cook:** 25 mins **Additional:** 1 hr **Total:** 1 hr 55 mins

Servings: 12

Yield: 1 9-inch layer cake

Ingredients

Cake:

- ½ cup shortening
- 1 ½ cups white sugar
- 2 large eggs eggs, room temperature
- 1 teaspoon butter flavored extract
- 4 tablespoons red food coloring
- 2 tablespoons unsweetened cocoa powder
- 1 cup buttermilk, room temperature
- 1 teaspoon salt
- 2 ½ cups sifted all-purpose flour
- 1 tablespoon white vinegar

- 1 teaspoon baking soda

Cream Cheese Frosting:

- ½ cup butter, room temperature
- 1 (8 ounce) package cream cheese, room temperature
- 4 cups confectioners' sugar, sifted
- 1 teaspoon vanilla extract

Directions

Step 1

Preheat oven to 350 degrees F (175 degrees C). Grease and flour two 9-inch round pans.

Step 2

Beat shortening and sugar until light and fluffy. Add eggs one at a time, mixing until fully incorporated. Stir in butter flavoring. Make a paste with food coloring and cocoa and add to the shortening mixture.

Step 3

Mix buttermilk, salt, baking soda and vinegar; add to batter alternating with the flour mixture.

Step 4

Divide batter into prepared pans. Bake in preheated oven until cake springs back when touched lightly with a finger or tester comes out clean, 20 to 30 minutes. Cook completely on wire rack.

Step 5

To Make Cream Cheese Frosting: beat butter and cream cheese with an electric mixer until smooth. Gradually beat in confectioners' sugar and 1 teaspoon vanilla. Mix until well blended.

Nutrition Facts

Per Serving:

579 calories; protein 6.1g 12% DV; carbohydrates 86.8g 28% DV; fat 24.1g 37% DV; cholesterol 72.7mg 24% DV; sodium 442.8mg 18% DV.

Maraschino Cherry Nut Cake

Prep: 30 mins **Cook:** 25 mins **Additional:** 1 hr 35 mins **Total:** 2 hrs 30 mins

Servings: 12

Yield: 1 9-inch cake

Ingredients

- 1 (10 ounce) jar maraschino cherries
- 2 ¼ cups sifted cake flour
- 2 ½ teaspoons baking powder
- ½ teaspoon salt, divided
- ½ cup shortening
- 1 ⅓ cups white sugar
- 3 large egg whites egg whites, room temperature
- ⅔ cup milk, room temperature
- ½ cup chopped pecans
- ¾ cup butter, room temperature
- 6 cups sifted confectioners' sugar, divided
- ⅓ cup milk
- 6 drops red food coloring
- 1 ½ teaspoons vanilla extract
- 12 cherries maraschino cherries, with stems

Directions

Step 1

Preheat oven to 350 degrees F (175 degrees C). Grease and lightly flour two 8- or 9-inch round cake pans or one 9x13-inch cake pan.

Step 2

Reserve 1/4 cup maraschino cherry juice. Coarsely chop the cherries to make 1/2 cup. Set aside.

Step 3

Sift cake flour, baking powder, and 1/4 teaspoon of the salt and set aside.

Step 4

Beat shortening in a large bowl with an electric mixer on medium high speed for 30 seconds. Add the 1 1/3 cups white sugar and beat until well combined. Add the egg whites, one at a time, beating well after each.

Step 5

Combine 2/3 cup milk and reserved 1/4 cup cherry juice. Add the flour and milk mixture alternately to the shortening mixture, beating on low speed after each addition until just combined. Stir in the chopped cherries and nuts. Pour batter into prepared pans.

Step 6

In preheated oven until cake springs back when lightly touched with a finger or a tester comes out clean, 20 to 25 minutes for round cakes (or 30 to 35 minutes for a 9x13 inch pan). Cool cakes in pans on a wire rack for 10 minutes, then invert onto wire rack to cool completely.

Step 7

To make frosting: beat 3/4 cups butter in a large bowl till fluffy. Gradually add 3 cups sifted confectioners' sugar; beat well. Slowly beat in 1/3 cup milk, 1 1/2 teaspoons vanilla, and remaining 1/4 teaspoon salt. Gradually beat in the remaining 3 cups sifted confectioners' sugar. Beat in additional milk (1 to 2 tablespoons) if needed, to make frosting of spreading consistency. If desired, tint the frosting pink by adding 6 drops of red food coloring.

Step 8

Once cake is completely cool, frost with butter frosting and decorate with maraschino cherries with stems.

Nutrition Facts

Per Serving:

676 calories; protein 4.4g 9% DV; carbohydrates 113.7g 37% DV; fat 24.1g 37% DV; cholesterol 32.1mg 11% DV; sodium 303.9mg 12% DV.

Deep Chocolate Raspberry Cake

Prep: 40 mins **Cook:** 45 mins **Additional:** 1 hr **Total:** 2 hrs 25 mins

Servings: 12

Yield: 1 9-inch layer cake

Ingredients

- 6 (1 ounce) squares semi-sweet chocolate
- 6 (1 ounce) squares unsweetened chocolate
- 7 large eggs eggs, separated
- 1 cup all-purpose flour
- 1 cup butter, room temperature
- 2 cups white sugar
- 1 ½ teaspoons vanilla extract
- 6 (1 ounce) squares semisweet chocolate

- ¾ cup heavy whipping cream
- 1 (4 ounce) package frozen raspberries, thawed

- 3 tablespoons seedless raspberry preserves

Directions

Step 1

Preheat oven to 300 degrees F (150 degrees C). Line bottoms of two 9-inch cake pans with parchment or waxed paper.

Step 2

To Make Cake: Melt 6 ounces of semisweet chocolate and 6 ounces of unsweetened chocolate in the top of a double boiler, or in a microwave. Cool, and beat in egg yolks.

Step 3

In a large bowl, beat butter, 1 1/2 cups sugar, and vanilla until light and fluffy. Add chocolate mixture, and continue beating until smooth. Stir in flour until just combined.

Step 4

In another bowl, beat egg whites until foamy. Gradually beat in 1/2 cup sugar, and continue beating until the whites hold soft peaks. Fold whites into chocolate batter, in three additions. Pour batter into prepared pans, and smooth tops.

Step 5

Bake in preheated oven until a toothpick stuck into the centers of the cakes comes out with moist crumbs, about 45 minutes. Cool in pans.

Step 6

To Make Frosting: In a saucepan, bring cream just to a boil. Chop 6 ounces semisweet chocolate, and stir into the cream. Remove saucepan from heat, and continue stirring until smooth. Pour frosting into bowl, and press sheet of plastic wrap directly against surface of chocolate to prevent a skin from forming. Refrigerate until thick enough to spread.

Step 7

To Make Filling: Drain the thawed raspberries, if necessary, and combine with the jam. Sandwich the cake layers with raspberry filling. Spread top and sides with chocolate frosting.

Nutrition Facts

Per Serving:

629 calories; protein 9.1g 18% DV; carbohydrates 67.9g 22% DV; fat 40.2g 62% DV; cholesterol 169.5mg 57% DV; sodium 159.2mg 6% DV.

White Chocolate Amaretto Cake

Prep: 30 mins **Cook:** 1 hr **Additional:** 2 hrs **Total:** 3 hrs 30 mins

Servings: 12

Yield: 1 (10 inch) Bundt cake

Ingredients

- 1 (18.25 ounce) package yellow cake mix
- 4 large eggs eggs
- 1 (3.3 ounce) package instant white chocolate pudding mix
- ½ cup cold water
- ½ cup vegetable oil
- ½ cup amaretto liqueur
- ¼ teaspoon almond extract
- ½ cup butter
- ¼ cup water
- 1 cup white sugar
- ½ cup amaretto liqueur
- 1 (16 ounce) package vanilla frosting
- ¼ cup blanched slivered almonds

Directions

Step 1

Preheat oven to 350 degrees F (175 degrees C). Lightly oil a 10 inch non-stick Bundt pan.

Step 2

In a large bowl, combine cake mix, eggs, pudding mix, 1/2 cup of cold water, oil, 1/2 cup amaretto and 1/4 teaspoon almond extract. Blend well for approximately 3 minutes.

Step 3

Pour batter into prepared 10 inch Bundt pan. Bake at 350 degrees F (175 degrees C) for 45 minutes to an hour, or until a toothpick inserted into the center of the cake comes out clean.

Step 4

Remove cake from oven, and use an ice pick or skewer to make as many holes as possible into the cake. Apply glaze while cake is still warm. Slowly and patiently drizzle glaze over cake, including the edges and center of Bundt pan. Allow cake to cool in the pan for at least 2 hours.

Step 5

To make the glaze: Combine butter, sugar, 1/4 cup water, and 1/2 cup amaretto in a saucepan. Bring to a boil, and continue to boil for 10 minutes, stirring constantly.

Step 6

Topping: Lightly toast slivered almonds in the oven. This will take 5 to 10 minutes. Stir frequently and be careful not to burn. Heat 1/4 cup of the prepared frosting in the microwave for 10 seconds, to soften. Place the cake on serving dish and use a spoon to drizzle the softened frosting over the cake. Scatter toasted almonds over cake before frosting cools.

Nutrition Facts

Per Serving:

681 calories; protein 4.8g 10% DV; carbohydrates 87.6g 28% DV; fat 31g 48% DV; cholesterol 83.5mg 28% DV; sodium 456.9mg 18% DV.

Southern Red Velvet Cake

Prep: 20 mins **Cook:** 25 mins **Additional:** 2 hrs **Total:** 2 hrs 45 mins

Servings: 16

Yield: 1 - 9 inch cake

Ingredients

- ½ cup shortening
- 1 ½ cups white sugar
- 2 large eggs eggs
- 1 teaspoon vanilla extract
- 1 teaspoon butter flavored extract
- 3 tablespoons cocoa powder
- ½ ounce red food coloring
- 2 ½ cups all-purpose flour
- 1 cup buttermilk
- 1 teaspoon salt
- 1 teaspoon baking soda
- 1 tablespoon distilled white vinegar
- 3 tablespoons all-purpose flour
- ½ teaspoon salt
- 1 cup milk
- ½ cup butter
- 1 cup white sugar
- ½ cup shortening
- 2 teaspoons vanilla extract
- 2 teaspoons butter flavored extract

Directions

Step 1

Preheat an oven to 350 degrees F (175 degrees C). Grease and flour three 10 inch round pans.

Step 2

Cream 1/2 cup of shortening, 1 1/2 cups of white sugar, eggs, 1 teaspoon of vanilla extract, and 1 teaspoon of butter flavored extract in a large bowl. Make a paste of cocoa and food coloring in a small bowl and add to shortening mixture. Pour in 2 1/2 cups flour alternately with the buttermilk, mixing until just incorporated. Mix 1 teaspoon of salt, baking soda, and vinegar in a small bowl, and while fizzing fold into the batter; mixing just enough to evenly combine. Pour the batter into prepared pan.

Step 3

Bake in the preheated oven until a toothpick inserted into the center comes out clean, 20 to 25 minutes. Cool in the pans for 10 minutes before removing to cool completely on a wire rack.

Step 4

To make frosting: Cook 3 tablespoons of flour, 1/2 teaspoon of salt, and milk in a skillet over low heat, stirring constantly, until thick. Let cool completely. Cream butter, 1 cup sugar, and 1/2 cup shortening in a separate bowl. Stir in 2 teaspoons each of vanilla extract and butter flavored extract. Then add flour mixture to bowl and cream together. Frost cooled cake.

Nutrition Facts

Per Serving:

390 calories; protein 4.2g 8% DV; carbohydrates 49.4g 16% DV; fat 19.9g 31% DV; cholesterol 40.3mg 13% DV; sodium 369.1mg 15% DV.

Valentine's Day Candy

Ruby Chocolate Rocky Road

Prep: 25 mins **Cook:** 5 mins **Additional:** 1 hr **Total:** 1 hr 30 mins

Servings: 20

Yield: 20 rocky road squares

Ingredients

- 14 ounces ruby chocolate, chopped
- ½ cup coconut oil
- 1 teaspoon vanilla extract
- 18 cookie (1-5/8" square)s shortbread cookies (such as Walkers), coarsely chopped
- ½ (10 ounce) package marshmallows, cut into cubes
- ½ cup shelled pistachio nuts
- ½ cup slivered almonds
- 1 ½ ounces candied flowers
- 3 tablespoons freeze-dried raspberries
- 3 tablespoons coconut flakes

Directions

Step 1

Grease a small baking sheet and line it with waxed paper.

Step 2

Place ruby chocolate, coconut oil, and vanilla extract in a large microwave-safe bowl. Microwave on full power until melted, about 1 1/2 minutes. Remove and stir vigorously with a silicone spatula. Press any remaining solid pieces of chocolate into the hot liquid until melted.

Step 3

Add shortbread cookies, marshmallows, pistachios, almonds, candied flowers, raspberries, and coconut flakes to the chocolate mixture. Stir gently until fully coated.

Step 4

Spread mixture on the prepared baking sheet and refrigerate until firm, 1 to 2 hours. Cut into squares using a really sharp knife.

Cook's Notes:

The reason I use the microwave with ruby chocolate is that it is easier to control the melting point. The color can go quickly if ruby chocolate is overheated. I also use plastic and silicone spatulas to work with all chocolate, as it doesn't keep the heat in the bowl itself, which also gives you more control.

Full power on my microwave is 900 watts.

Nutrition Facts

Per Serving:

266 calories; protein 4g 8% DV; carbohydrates 25g 8% DV; fat 17.4g 27% DV; cholesterol 4.9mg 2% DV; sodium 72.8mg 3% DV.

Nipples of Venus (Capezzoli di Venere)

Prep: 1 hr **Cook:** 10 mins **Total:** 1 hr 10 mins

Servings: 24

Yield: 24 truffles

Ingredients

- ⅓ cup white sugar
- 5 tablespoons unsalted butter, room temperature
- 6 ounces dark chocolate, chopped
- 14 ounces whole chestnuts
- 1 pinch salt
- 1 pinch cayenne pepper
- 1 teaspoon vanilla extract
- ¼ cup brandy
- 8 ounces white chocolate, chopped
- ⅓ cup confectioners' sugar
- 2 teaspoons milk, or as needed
- paper candy cups
- 1 drop red food coloring, or more as needed

Directions

Step 1

Cream sugar and butter together with a spatula until light and creamy. Set aside.

Step 2

Heat an inch of water in a pot set over low heat. Melt dark chocolate in a heat-proof bowl placed over the pot. Stir with a small spatula.

Step 3

Place chestnuts in a food processor; pulse on and off until very finely ground. Add chestnuts to the sugar-butter mixture and stir until combined. Add salt, cayenne pepper, vanilla extract, and brandy. Stir well. Pour in the melted chocolate and mix again until filling is well blended.

Step 4

Scoop filling onto a silicone-lined baking sheet and smooth out if necessary. Cover the balls in plastic wrap and refrigerate while you prepare the white chocolate coating.

Step 5

Reserve about 20% of the white chocolate to stir in later. Melt the rest in a heat-proof bowl over a pot of simmering water until an instant-read thermometer inserted in to the chocolate reads 105 degree F (41 degrees C). Add the reserved white chocolate and stir until melted.

Step 6

Place 1 chocolate truffle on a fork and hold it up above the white chocolate coating. Spoon on the white chocolate until ball is well coated. Use another fork to push the truffle onto a lined baking sheet. Repeat with the remaining truffles and coating. Place the bowl of coating back over hot water if it chocolate starts to harden.

Step 7

Mix confectioners' sugar with enough milk to make a very thick paste that will hold together well. Dye it pink with red food coloring. Transfer into a piping bag and pipe a small dot on top of each truffle. Serve truffles in paper candy cups.

Nutrition Facts

Per Serving:

169 calories; protein 1.4g 3% DV; carbohydrates 21.3g 7% DV; fat 8.2g 13% DV; cholesterol 8.7mg 3% DV; sodium 17.6mg 1% DV.

Ultimate Valentine's Day Chocolate Truffle

Servings: 2

Yield: 2 servings

Ingredients

- 4 ½ ounces semisweet chocolate, chopped
- 2 ½ ounces unsalted butter, softened
- 1 egg yolk
- 4 ounces sifted confectioners' sugar

- 3 ounces heavy cream
- 1 tablespoon coffee-flavored liqueur
- 4 ounces semisweet chocolate, chopped
- powdered gold leaf

Directions

Step 1

Melt 4.5 ounces of the semi-sweet chocolate in a double boiler until just fluid. Using a whisk, incorporate softened butter, then egg yolk, sifted sugar and cream into the melted chocolate. Whisk until smooth.

Step 2

Pour chocolate mixture in heart molds or any other molds (an egg poacher works well as a mold), and refrigerate until set, about 3 hours.

Step 3

Melt remaining 4 ounces of chocolate in a double boiler until just fluid.

Step 4

Unmold chocolate truffles and dip them in the melted chocolate, shake off excess chocolate and leave to set on parchment paper. Trim excess chocolate.

Step 5

In a small bowl, combine liqueur and gold dust to achieve a paint-like consistency. Using brushes, decorate hearts with gold "paint" A simple "I love You" is quite effective, or better still use an original romantic quote. If you are very artistic, birds, or a floral motif along the edges complete the effect.

Nutrition Facts

Per Serving:

1264 calories; protein 11g 22% DV; carbohydrates 128.6g 42% DV; fat 84.7g 130% DV; cholesterol 236mg 79% DV; sodium 25.1mg 1% DV.

Mocha Truffles

Prep: 30 mins **Cook:** 5 mins **Additional:** 2 hrs **Total:** 2 hrs 35 mins

Servings: 66

Yield: 5 1/2 dozen truffles

Ingredients

Truffle:

- 1 (24 ounce) bag semi-sweet chocolate chips
- 8 ounces cream cheese, softened

- 3 tablespoons instant coffee granules
- 2 teaspoons water

Coating:

- 6 ounces semi-sweet chocolate chips

- 1 tablespoon shortening

Directions

Step 1

Line a baking sheet with waxed paper.

Step 2

Melt 24 ounces chocolate chips in a microwave-safe glass or ceramic bowl in 30-second intervals, stirring after each melting, 1 to 3 minutes. Mix cream cheese, coffee granules, and water into melted chocolate until smooth. Chill chocolate mixture until firm enough to shape, about 30 minutes.

Step 3

Shape chocolate mixture into 1-inch balls and place on the prepared baking sheet. Chill truffles until firm, at least 1 to 2 hours.

Step 4

Melt 6 ounces chocolate chips and shortening in a microwave-safe glass or ceramic bowl in 30-second intervals, stirring after each melting, for 1 to 3 minutes.

Step 5

Dip truffles in the melted chocolate mixture and return to the waxed paper. Set aside until firm, at least 30 minutes.

Cook's Notes:

White or milk chocolate chips can be used in place of the semi-sweet for the coating.

Nutrition Facts

Per Serving:

76 calories; protein 0.9g 2% DV; carbohydrates 8g 3% DV; fat 5.3g 8% DV; cholesterol 3.8mg 1% DV; sodium 11.3mg 1% DV.

Hazelnut Cups

Prep: 30 mins **Cook:** 2 mins **Additional:** 4 hrs 30 mins **Total:** 5 hrs 2 mins

Servings: 8

Yield: 24 individual cups

Ingredients

Chocolate Shells:

- 1 ¼ cups bittersweet chocolate chips
- 1 teaspoon vegetable oil
- Filling:
- 1 cup heavy cream
- 1 teaspoon vanilla extract
- 3 tablespoons coffee flavored liqueur (such as Kahlua)
- 2 teaspoons white sugar
- ½ cup chocolate-hazelnut spread (such as Nutella)

Garnish:

- ½ cup heavy cream
- 1 teaspoon white sugar
- 2 tablespoons chopped hazelnuts, for garnish
- 24 eaches chocolate-covered coffee beans

Directions

Step 1

Combine the chocolate chips and oil in a microwave-safe measuring cup or ceramic bowl. Stir until all of the chips are coated with oil. Microwave for 1 minute at 60% power. Stir. Heat at full power at 15-second intervals until the chocolate is melted, stirring after every interval. (This will take between 1 to 3 minutes, depending on your microwave.)

Step 2

Arrange 24 paper bonbon or candy cups on a baking sheet. Pour a small amount (about 2 teaspoons) of the melted chocolate mixture into each cup. Tip the cups to coat the insides fully with chocolate. Transfer the coated cups to the refrigerator. Reserve remaining chocolate.

Step 3

Pour the cup of heavy cream, vanilla extract, and coffee liqueur in a mixing bowl. Beat on high speed until frothy. Add the 2 teaspoons of sugar and continue to beat on high until soft peaks form. Stir in the hazelnut spread and beat on medium speed until combined. Quickly fold in the reserved melted chocolate. (If the chocolate has started to set up, place in microwave again for 10 seconds at 60% power.)

Step 4

Fill a pastry bag with the mousse filling and pipe it into each chocolate cup. (If a pastry bag is unavailable, use a resealable plastic storage bag and snip off a corner.) You may need to use a spoon to smooth the tops. Chill the filled shells in the refrigerator for at least 4 hours.

Step 5

Whip the 1/2 cup of cream until frothy; add the teaspoon of sugar and whip until stiff peaks form. Use a pastry bag to top each chocolate cup with a small dollop of whipped cream. Sprinkle with chopped hazelnuts and top with a coffee bean. Refrigerate until serving.

Cook's Notes

The chocolate cups can be made up to one day in advance of serving. Store them in an airtight container in the refrigerator.

Whole hazelnut-flavored coffee beans can be used instead of chocolate-covered coffee beans, if desired.

Nutrition Facts

Per Serving:

463 calories; protein 3.7g 8% DV; carbohydrates 38.7g 13% DV; fat 34.4g 53% DV; cholesterol 61.7mg 21% DV; sodium 36.1mg 1% DV.

Easy OREO Truffles

Additional: 1 hr 30 mins **Total:** 1 hr 30 mins

Servings: 42

Yield: 3 -1/2 dozen

Ingredients

- 1 (16 ounce) package OREO Chocolate Sandwich Cookies, divided
- 1 (8 ounce) package PHILADELPHIA Cream Cheese, softened
- 2 (8 ounce) packages BAKER'S Semi-Sweet Baking Chocolate, melted

Directions

Step 1

Crush 9 of the cookies to fine crumbs in food processor; reserve for later use. (Cookies can also be finely crushed in a resealable plastic bag using a rolling pin.) Crush remaining 36 cookies to fine crumbs; place in medium bowl. Add cream cheese; mix until well blended. Roll cookie mixture into 42 balls, about 1-inch in diameter.

Step 2

Dip balls in chocolate; place on wax paper-covered baking sheet. (Any leftover chocolate can be stored at room temperature for another use.) Sprinkle with reserved cookie crumbs.

Step 3

Refrigerate until firm, about 1 hour. Store leftover truffles, covered, in refrigerator.

Caramels

Servings: 60

Yield: 4 to 5 dozen caramels

Ingredients

- 2 cups white sugar
- 1 cup packed brown sugar
- 1 cup corn syrup
- 1 cup evaporated milk
- 1 pint heavy whipping cream
- 1 cup butter
- 1 ¼ teaspoons vanilla extract

Directions

Step 1

Grease a 12x15 inch pan.

Step 2

In a medium-size pot, combine sugar, brown sugar, corn syrup, evaporated milk, whipping cream, and butter. Monitor the heat of the mixture with a candy thermometer while stirring. When the thermometer reaches 250 degrees F (120 degrees C) remove the pot from the heat.

Step 3

Stir in vanilla. Transfer mixture to the prepared pan and let the mixture cool completely. When cooled cut the Carmel into small squares and wrap them in wax paper for storage.

Nutrition Facts

Per Serving:

115 calories; protein 0.5g 1% DV; carbohydrates 14.8g 5% DV; fat 6.3g 10% DV; cholesterol 20.2mg 7% DV; sodium 30.4mg 1% DV.

Pralines

Cook: 30 mins **Additional:** 15 mins **Total:** 45 mins

Servings: 20

Yield: 20 servings

Ingredients

- 1 ½ cups toasted pecans
- 1 ½ cups white sugar
- ⅜ cup butter
- ¾ cup brown sugar
- ½ cup milk
- 1 teaspoon vanilla extract

Directions

Step 1

Line a baking sheet with aluminum foil.

Step 2

In large saucepan over medium heat, combine pecans, sugar, butter, brown sugar, milk and vanilla. Heat to between 234 and 240 degrees F (112 to 116 degrees C), or until a small amount of syrup dropped into cold water forms a soft ball that flattens when removed from the water and placed on a flat surface.

Step 3

Drop by spoonfuls onto prepared baking sheet. Let cool completely.

Nutrition Facts

Per Serving:

180 calories; protein 1g 2% DV; carbohydrates 24.5g 8% DV; fat 9.4g 15% DV; cholesterol 9.6mg 3% DV; sodium 29.3mg 1% DV.

Easy Decadent Truffles

Prep: 1 hr **Total:** 1 hr

Servings: 60

Yield: 5 dozen

Ingredients

- 1 (8 ounce) package cream cheese, softened
- 3 cups confectioners' sugar, sifted
- 3 cups semisweet chocolate chips, melted
- 1 ½ teaspoons vanilla

Directions

Step 1

In a large bowl, beat cream cheese until smooth. Gradually beat in confectioners' sugar until well blended. Stir in melted chocolate and vanilla until no streaks remain. Refrigerate for about 1 hour. Shape into 1 inch balls.

Notes

Roll truffles in ground walnuts (or any ground nuts), cocoa, coconut, confectioners' sugar, candy sprinkles, etc.

To flavor truffles with liqueurs or other flavorings, omit vanilla. Divide truffle mixture into thirds. Add 1 tablespoon liqueur (almond, coffee, orange) to each mixture; mix well.

Chocolate Covered Cherries

Prep: 1 hr **Total:** 1 hr

Servings: 60

Yield: 60 pieces

Ingredients

- 60 cherries maraschino cherries with stems
- 3 tablespoons butter, softened
- 3 tablespoons corn syrup
- 2 cups sifted confectioners' sugar
- 1 pound chocolate confectioners' coating

Directions

Step 1

Drain cherries and set on paper towels to dry.

Step 2

In a medium bowl, combine butter and corn syrup until smooth. Stir in confectioners' sugar and knead to form a dough. Chill to stiffen if necessary. Wrap each cherry in about 1 teaspoon of dough. Chill until firm.

Step 3

Melt confectioners' coating in a heavy saucepan over low heat. Dip each cherry in by its stem, and place on waxed paper lined sheets. Chill until completely set. Store in an airtight container in a cool place. Best after 1 or 2 weeks.

Nutrition Facts

Per Serving:

68 calories; protein 0.6g 1% DV; carbohydrates 10.5g 3% DV; fat 3.6g 6% DV; cholesterol 1.5mg 1% DV; sodium 5.1mg.

Melt In Your Mouth Toffee

Prep: 10 mins **Cook:** 20 mins **Additional:** 30 mins **Total:** 1 hr

Servings: 48

Yield: 48 servings

Ingredients

- 1 pound butter
- 1 cup white sugar
- 1 cup packed brown sugar
- 1 cup chopped walnuts
- 2 cups semisweet chocolate chips

Directions

Step 1

In a heavy saucepan, combine butter, white sugar, and brown sugar. Cook over medium heat, stirring constantly until mixture boils. Boil to brittle stage, 300 degrees F (150 degrees C) without stirring. Remove from heat.

Step 2

Pour nuts and chocolate chips into a 9x13 inch dish. Pour hot mixture over the nuts and chocolate. Let the mixture cool and break it into pieces before serving.

Nutrition Facts

Per Serving:

153 calories; protein 1g 2% DV; carbohydrates 13.6g 4% DV; fat 11.3g 17% DV; cholesterol 20.3mg 7% DV; sodium 55.8mg 2% DV.

Rum Truffles

Prep: 10 mins **Cook:** 10 mins **Additional:** 1 hr 30 mins **Total:** 1 hr 50 mins

Servings: 24

Yield: 24 truffles

Ingredients

- 8 (1 ounce) squares bittersweet chocolate, chopped
- ¼ cup cream
- 2 tablespoons unsalted butter

- ½ cup chocolate cake crumbs
- 2 teaspoons dark rum
- ½ cup chocolate sprinkles

Directions

Step 1

Line a sheet pan with aluminum foil or parchment paper. Place chopped chocolate in a heatproof bowl.

Step 2

In a saucepan, combine cream and butter. Place over low heat, and bring to a boil. Pour over chocolate, and stir until chocolate is melted and smooth. Stir in cake crumbs and rum. Set aside until firm, but not hard.

Step 3

Roll heaping teaspoons of chocolate mixture into balls, then roll in the chocolate sprinkles. Place on the prepared tray. Refrigerate 30 minutes or until firm. Serve in small paper cups.

Note

I save up chocolate cake crumbs whenever I have a chance. They can be stored in the freezer. Pack the crumbs in the amount needed. A good chocolate cake makes all the difference!

Nutrition Facts

Per Serving:

98 calories; protein 0.9g 2% DV; carbohydrates 9.6g 3% DV; fat 6.2g 10% DV; cholesterol 7.7mg 3% DV; sodium 9.2mg.

Strawberry Heart Bark

Prep: 15 mins **Cook:** 2 mins **Additional:** 50 mins **Total:** 1 hr 7 mins

Servings: 12

Yield: 12 servings

Ingredients

- 8 ounces semisweet chocolate, chopped
- 8 ounces white chocolate, chopped
- ½ cup conversation heart candies (such as Necco)
- ¾ cup freeze-dried strawberries

- 1 tablespoon pink sprinkles, or to taste

Directions

Step 1

Melt semisweet chocolate in a microwave-safe bowl in 15-second intervals, stirring after each melting, 1 to 3 minutes.

Step 2

Melt white chocolate in a separate microwave-safe bowl in 15-second intervals, stirring after each melting, 1 to 3 minutes.

Step 3

Line a baking sheet with parchment paper. Pour semisweet chocolate on the parchment paper; spread into a large rectangle. Drizzle white chocolate over the semisweet chocolate in lines and zigzags. Swirl chocolates together into a marble pattern using a toothpick or skewer.

Step 4

Scatter conversation heart candies over chocolate. Scatter freeze-dried strawberries and pink sprinkles in the remaining gaps. Let stand at room temperature for about 20 minutes.

Step 5

Refrigerate chocolate bark until firm, about 30 minutes. Break into large chunks.

Nutrition Facts

Per Serving:

224 calories; protein 2.5g 5% DV; carbohydrates 28.6g 9% DV; fat 12.2g 19% DV; cholesterol 3.9mg 1% DV; sodium 18.8mg 1% DV.

Homemade Valentine's Chocolates

Prep: 15 mins **Cook:** 5 mins **Additional:** 30 mins **Total:** 50 mins

Servings: 32

Yield: 32 truffles

Ingredients

- ½ pound high-quality dark chocolate,
  chopped
- ⅛ teaspoon ground dried chipotle pepper
- 1 pinch salt
- ½ cup heavy whipping cream
- 3 tablespoons unsweetened cocoa powder,
  or as needed

Directions

Step 1

Place chocolate into a bowl; add chipotle pepper and salt.

Step 2

Heat cream in a small saucepan over medium-low heat until it comes to a boil. Pour cream over chocolate and let stand for 3 minutes.

Step 3

Stir gently until chocolate mixture is completely smooth. Pour chocolate mixture out onto a sheet of plastic wrap on a work surface. Pick up one edge of the plastic and roll the chocolate into a rough log shape. Continue to roll, wrapping chocolate in the plastic. Refrigerate until chilled and firm, 30 minutes to 1 hour.

Step 4

Place cocoa into a small bowl. Unwrap chocolate and cut in half crosswise; cut each half into halves lengthwise. Roughly cut candy into 1/2-inch square 'stones'. Place the chocolate pieces into the cocoa and toss gently to coat.

Nutrition Facts

Per Serving:

48 calories; protein 0.5g 1% DV; carbohydrates 4.9g 2% DV; fat 3.6g 6% DV; cholesterol 5.1mg 2% DV; sodium 2.3mg.

Cherries and Chocolate Fudge

Prep: 10 mins **Cook:** 3 mins **Additional:** 2 hrs **Total:** 2 hrs 13 mins

Servings: 60

Yield: 60 pieces

Ingredients

- 1 (14 ounce) can sweetened condensed milk
- 1 (12 ounce) package semisweet chocolate chips
- ½ cup chopped almonds
- ½ cup chopped candied cherries
- 1 teaspoon almond extract
- ¼ cup pecan halves
- ¼ cup candied cherries, halved

Directions

Step 1

Line an 8 x 8 inch square pan with aluminum foil.

Step 2

In a microwave-safe bowl combine sweetened condensed milk and chocolate chips; microwave on high for 1 1/2 minutes, or until chocolate is melted. Stir until smooth. Stir in chopped almonds, chopped cherries and almond extract. Pour into prepared pan and spread evenly. Place pecan halves and cherry halves on top.

Step 3

Cover and refrigerate for 2 hours, or until firm. Cut into 1 inch squares. Store, covered, in refrigerator.

Nutrition Facts

Per Serving:

61 calories; protein 1g 2% DV; carbohydrates 8.6g 3% DV; fat 3g 5% DV; cholesterol 2.2mg 1% DV; sodium 10.2mg.

Double-Decker Marshmallow Fudge

Prep: 30 mins **Cook:** 17 mins **Additional:** 10 hrs 15 mins **Total:** 11 hrs 2 mins

Servings: 24

Yield: 1 9x13-inch pan

Ingredients

- cooking spray
- ¼ cup butter
- 1 (14 ounce) can sweetened condensed milk
- 3 cups semisweet chocolate chips
- ½ cup cold water
- 3 (.25 ounce) packages unflavored gelatin
- 2 cups white sugar

- ½ cup water

- 1 cup confectioners' sugar

Directions

Step 1

Line a 9x13-inch cake or jelly roll pan with aluminum foil; coat with cooking spray.

Step 2

Melt butter in a medium saucepan over medium heat; stir in condensed milk. Pour in chocolate chips; cook and stir until melted, 5 to 10 minutes.

Step 3

Pour chocolate mixture into the prepared pan. Coat a spatula with cooking spray and use to press chocolate mixture into an even layer. Refrigerate fudge until cooled and set, about 2 hours.

Step 4

Combine 1/2 cup cold water and gelatin in a bowl; set aside until gelatin starts to thicken, about 15 minutes.

Step 5

Mix white sugar and 1/2 cup water in a saucepan over medium heat; cook and stir until sugar dissolves, 5 to 8 minutes. Bring sugar mixture to a boil and cook until temperature reaches 240 degrees F (116 degrees C) on a candy thermometer, 2 to 3 minutes. Remove from heat.

Step 6

Slowly pour sugar mixture into gelatin mixture while simultaneously beating with an electric mixer set on low. Gradually increase speed to high and continue beating until marshmallow batter is very thick but not stiff, 10 to 15 minutes.

Step 7

Pour marshmallow batter over fudge, smoothing the surface with spatula coated with cooking spray. Let sit uncovered at room temperature until completely set, about 6 hours.

Step 8

Dust the top of marshmallow layer with most of the confectioners' sugar. Refrigerate marshmallow fudge for at least 2 hours.

Step 9

Lift marshmallow fudge out of the pan by the edges of the foil and place on a large cutting board. Dip a large knife in the remaining confectioners' sugar and slice fudge into 1 1/2-inch squares, continually dipping knife in the sugar after each slice.

Cook's Note:

A standing mixer will speed up the process in Step 5 a lot, so keep an eye on it so it doesn't get so thick you can't pour it.

Nutrition Facts

Per Serving:

258 calories; protein 2.9g 6% DV; carbohydrates 44g 14% DV; fat 9.6g 15% DV; cholesterol 10.6mg 4% DV; sodium 38.9mg 2% DV.

Basic Truffles

Prep: 10 mins **Cook:** 10 mins **Additional:** 1 hr 30 mins **Total:** 1 hr 50 mins

Servings: 35

Yield: 35 truffles

Ingredients

- 12 ounces bittersweet chocolate, chopped
- ⅓ cup heavy cream
- 1 teaspoon vanilla extract

Directions

Step 1

In a medium saucepan over medium heat, combine chocolate and cream. Cook, stirring, until chocolate is melted and mixture is smooth. Remove from heat and whisk in flavoring. Pour into a small dish and refrigerate until set, but not hard, 1 1/2 to 2 hours. Use to fill candies or form balls and roll in toppings.

Nutrition Facts

Per Serving:

62 calories; protein 0.7g 1% DV; carbohydrates 5.6g 2% DV; fat 4.1g 6% DV; cholesterol 3.5mg 1% DV; sodium 1.4mg.

Cherry Mash Candy

Prep: 10 mins **Cook:** 10 mins **Additional:** 40 mins **Total:** 1 hr

Servings: 12

Yield: 1 9x13 inch pan

Ingredients

- 2 cups white sugar
- ⅔ cup evaporated milk
- 1 ¼ cups miniature marshmallows
- ½ cup butter
- 1 dash salt
- 1 ¼ cups cherry baking chips
- 1 teaspoon vanilla extract
- 2 cups semisweet chocolate chips
- ¾ cup chunky peanut butter

Directions

Step 1

In a large saucepan over medium heat, stir together sugar, milk, marshmallows, butter, and salt. Simmer for about 5 minutes or until mixture reaches soft ball stage, 240 degrees F (115 degrees C). Turn off heat. Add cherry chips and vanilla; stir until melted.

Step 2

Pour mixture into a well-greased 9x13 inch pan, and let cool until firm.

Step 3

In a microwave, or in a saucepan over low heat, melt chocolate chips and peanut butter. Pour over cherry mixture and spread evenly. Allow to cool completely before cutting.

Nutrition Facts

Per Serving:

558 calories; protein 7.3g 15% DV; carbohydrates 71.9g 23% DV; fat 29.8g 46% DV; cholesterol 24.4mg 8% DV; sodium 189.6mg 8% DV.

Chocolate Orange Truffles

Prep: 40 mins **Cook:** 20 mins **Additional:** 4 hrs 30 mins **Total:** 5 hrs 30 mins

Servings: 12

Yield: 2 dozen

Ingredients

- ¼ cup unsalted butter
- 3 tablespoons heavy cream
- 4 (1 ounce) squares semisweet chocolate, chopped
- 2 tablespoons orange liqueur
- 1 teaspoon grated orange zest
- 4 (1 ounce) squares semisweet chocolate, chopped
- 1 tablespoon vegetable oil

Directions

Step 1

In a medium saucepan over medium-high heat, combine butter and cream. Bring to a boil, and remove from heat. Stir in 4 ounces chopped chocolate, orange liqueur, and orange zest; continue stirring until smooth. Pour truffle mixture into a shallow bowl or a 9X5 in loaf pan. Chill until firm, about 2 hours.

Step 2

Line a baking sheet with waxed paper. Shape chilled truffle mixture by rounded teaspoons into small balls (a melon baller also works well for this part). Place on prepared baking sheet. Chill until firm, about 30 minutes.

Step 3

In the top of a double boiler over lightly simmering water, melt remaining 4 ounces chocolate with the oil, stirring until smooth. Cool to lukewarm.

Step 4

Drop truffles, one at a time, into melted chocolate mixture. Using 2 forks, lift truffles out of the chocolate, allowing any excess chocolate to drip back into the pan before transferring back onto baking sheet. Chill until set.

Nutrition Facts

Per Serving:

159 calories; protein 1.5g 3% DV; carbohydrates 11.8g 4% DV; fat 12.4g 19% DV; cholesterol 15.3mg 5% DV; sodium 2.1mg.

Chocolate Orange Fondue

Prep: 10 mins **Cook:** 5 mins **Total:** 15 mins

Servings: 6

Yield: 6 servings

Ingredients

- 1 ¼ cups heavy cream
- 3 tablespoons freshly squeezed orange juice
- 12 ounces dark chocolate, chopped
- 1 tablespoon grated orange zest
- 1 teaspoon orange liqueur

Directions

Step 1

Heat the cream and orange juice in a saucepan over medium heat until it starts to bubble at the edges. Remove from the heat, and immediately whisk in the chocolate, orange zest, and orange liqueur until smooth. Serve in a fondue pot over the lowest heat setting, or farthest from the heat source.

Nutrition Facts

Per Serving:

491 calories; protein 4.9g 10% DV; carbohydrates 34.8g 11% DV; fat 37.2g 57% DV; cholesterol 70.3mg 23% DV; sodium 21.9mg 1% DV.

Coconut Ice

Prep: 5 mins **Cook:** 30 mins **Additional:** 55 mins **Total:** 1 hr 30 mins

Servings: 20

Yield: 1 - 7x7 inch pan

Ingredients

- 2 cups white sugar
- .66 cup water

- 1 teaspoon vanilla extract
- 1 ⅓ cups flaked coconut
- 2 drops red food coloring

Directions

Step 1

Line a 7 x 7 inch pan with parchment or waxed paper. In a medium, heavy-bottomed saucepan, heat sugar and water gently, without boiling, until sugar has dissolved. Then, bring to a boil and cook until it reaches 240 degrees F/120 degrees C on a candy thermometer, or a little syrup dropped in a glass of cold water forms a soft ball.

Step 2

Remove from heat and immediately stir in vanilla and coconut. Continue stirring until mixture begins to thicken, 5 to 10 minutes.

Step 3

Pour half of the mixture into the prepared pan and level the surface with a knife or spatula. Tint the other half of the mixture by stirring in the food coloring. Pour the pink mixture on top of other layer, and level the surface. Press all down firmly with the back of a spoon and allow to harden. When firm, turn out of the pan, remove the paper and cut into squares with a sharp knife.

Nutrition Facts

Per Serving:

119 calories; protein 0.4g 1% DV; carbohydrates 21.5g 7% DV; fat 4g 6% DV; cholesterolmg; sodium 2.3mg.

Twilight Dark Chocolate Truffles

Prep: 5 mins **Cook:** 10 mins **Additional:** 1 hr 20 mins **Total:** 1 hr 35 mins

Servings: 45

Yield: 45 truffles

Ingredients

- 1 cup heavy cream
- 2 tablespoons butter
- 4 (1 ounce) squares baking chocolate
- 2 ¾ cups semi-sweet chocolate chips
- 2 tablespoons instant espresso powder

Directions

Step 1

Combine the heavy cream, butter, baking chocolate, chocolate chips, and espresso powder in a saucepan over medium heat; stirring constantly, cook until the chocolate has melted into a smooth and thick mixture. Remove from heat. Pour into a bowl and chill in refrigerator until the mixture hardens, about 1 hour

Step 2

Line a baking sheet with waxed paper. Scoop small balls of the chocolate mixture onto the waxed paper. Store in refrigerator until the balls harden completely. Store in a cool, dry place.

Nutrition Facts

Per Serving:

87 calories; protein 1.2g 2% DV; carbohydrates 6.8g 2% DV; fat 7.1g 11% DV; cholesterol 8.6mg 3% DV; sodium 6.3mg.

Easy Chocolate Chip Cookie Dough Truffles

Prep: 1 hr 30 mins **Total:** 1 hr 30 mins

Servings: 48

Yield: 48 truffles

Ingredients

- ½ cup butter, softened
- ¾ cup packed brown sugar
- 1 teaspoon vanilla extract
- 2 ¼ cups all-purpose flour
- 1 (14 ounce) can sweetened condensed milk
- ½ cup miniature semisweet chocolate chips
- ½ cup toffee baking bits
- 1 pound chocolate confectioners' coating

Directions

Step 1

Beat the butter and brown sugar with an electric mixer in a large bowl until smooth. Beat in the vanilla extract. Add flour, alternately with sweetened condensed milk, beating well after each addition. Fold in the chocolate chips and toffee bits; mixing just enough to evenly combine.

Step 2

Using a small cookie scoop, make 1-inch balls and place them on waxed paper lined baking sheets. Refrigerate until firm, about 1 hour.

Step 3

Melt the chocolate coating in a microwave-safe glass or ceramic bowl in 30-second intervals, stirring after each melting, for 1 to 3 minutes (depending on your microwave). Do not overheat or coating will scorch. Dip the dough balls in the chocolate coating, allowing any excess to drip off. Place on waxed-paper lined baking sheets and sprinkle the truffles with additional toffee pieces. Refrigerate until firm, about 15 minutes. Store in the refrigerator.

Nutrition Facts

Per Serving:

146 calories; protein 2.1g 4% DV; carbohydrates 19.3g 6% DV; fat 7.9g 12% DV; cholesterol 9.9mg 3% DV; sodium 37.8mg 2% DV.

White Chocolate Grapes

Prep: 20 mins **Cook:** 2 mins **Total:** 22 mins

Servings: 20

Yield: 20 servings

Ingredients

- 2 cups white chocolate chips
- 2 teaspoons shortening
- 1 pound seedless grapes
- 1 cup finely chopped salted peanuts

Directions

Step 1

Combine the white chocolate chips and shortening in a small microwave-safe bowl. Heat in the microwave for 30 second intervals, stirring between each, until melted and smooth. Spread the chopped peanuts out on a piece of waxed paper or a dinner plate.

Step 2

Dip clean, dry grapes into the chocolate, then roll in the peanuts. Set on waxed paper until dry. Warm chocolate as needed in the microwave to keep it liquid.

Nutrition Facts

Milk Chocolate Peppermint Bark

Prep: 30 mins **Additional:** 1 hr 30 mins **Total:** 2 hrs

Servings: 50

Yield: 3 1/2 pounds

Ingredients

- 2 (12 ounce) packages milk chocolate chips
- 2 (12 ounce) packages white chocolate chips
- 2 teaspoons peppermint extract
- 8 eaches peppermint candy canes, crushed, divided

Directions

Step 1

Line a 12x18 inch jelly roll pan with aluminum foil.

Step 2

Melt the milk chocolate in a microwave-safe glass or ceramic bowl in 30-second intervals, stirring after each melting, for 1 to 5 minutes (depending on your microwave). Do not overheat or chocolate will scorch. Stir in the peppermint extract. Spread the chocolate evenly in the prepared pan; chill until set, about 30 minutes.

Step 3

Meanwhile, melt the white chocolate in a microwave-safe glass or ceramic bowl in 30-second intervals, stirring after each melting, for 1 to 5 minutes. Stir in 1/4 cup of the crushed candy canes. Spread the white chocolate mixture evenly over the milk chocolate. Sprinkle the remaining candy cane pieces evenly over the white chocolate layer. Chill until set, about 1 hour. Break into small pieces to serve.

Nutrition Facts

Per Serving:

167 calories; protein 1.9g 4% DV; carbohydrates 20.2g 7% DV; fat 9.3g 14% DV; cholesterol 7.4mg 3% DV; sodium 38.8mg 2% DV.

Dark Chocolate Cabernet Truffles

Prep: 20 mins **Additional:** 2 hrs 10 mins **Total:** 2 hrs 30 mins

Servings: 12

Yield: 2 dozen truffles

Ingredients

- ⅓ cup heavy whipping cream
- ½ teaspoon vanilla extract
- 1 pinch salt
- 2 tablespoons Cabernet Sauvignon wine
- 6 (1 ounce) squares semisweet chocolate, chopped
- 1 tablespoon unsalted butter, room temperature
- ¼ cup unsweetened cocoa powder

Directions

Step 1

Combine cream, vanilla extract, and salt together in a saucepan; bring to a boil. Stir wine into cream mixture and remove from heat.

Step 2

Stir semisweet chocolate into cream mixture until completely melted. Stir butter into mixture until incorporated. Pour chocolate mixture into a container, cover with plastic wrap, and refrigerate until firm, at least 2 hours.

Step 3

Line 2 baking sheets with parchment paper.

Step 4

Scoop the chocolate mixture using a teaspoon or a melon baller and shape into 1-inch balls. Place balls on the prepared baking sheets and refrigerate for 10 minutes.

Step 5

Remove from refrigerator and roll balls in cocoa powder to coat.

Nutrition Facts

Per Serving:

108 calories; protein 1.5g 3% DV; carbohydrates 9.2g 3% DV; fat 8.2g 13% DV; cholesterol 11.6mg 4% DV; sodium 3.1mg.

Cherry-Pistachio Bark

Prep: 15 mins **Cook:** 7 mins **Additional:** 1 hr **Total:** 1 hr 22 mins

Servings: 150

Yield: 3 1/2 pounds

Ingredients

- 1 ¼ cups dried cherries
- 2 tablespoons water
- 2 (11 ounce) packages white chocolate chips
- 4 (3 ounce) bars vanilla-flavored candy coating
- 1 ¼ cups chopped pistachio nuts

Directions

Step 1

In a small glass bowl, microwave cherries with water on high for 2 minutes; drain, and set aside.

Step 2

In a separate microwave-safe bowl, microwave chocolate chips and candy coating together until melted and smooth, stirring occasionally. Stir in cherries and chopped pistachios, and spread into a wax paper-lined 15x10 inch pan. Chill for 1 hour, or until firm.

Step 3

Cut into 1 inch squares, and enjoy. Store unused portion in an air-tight container.

Nutrition Facts

Per Serving:

45 calories; protein 0.7g 1% DV; carbohydrates 4.8g 2% DV; fat 2.6g 4% DV; cholesterol 1.3mg; sodium 10.9mg.

Irish Cream Truffles

Prep: 15 mins **Cook:** 10 mins **Additional:** 1 hr **Total:** 1 hr 25 mins

Servings: 24

Yield: 2 dozen truffles

Ingredients

- 1 cup heavy cream
- ¼ cup white sugar
- ¼ cup butter
- 1 (16 ounce) package semisweet chocolate chips
- 1 tablespoon Irish cream liqueur

Directions

Step 1

Whisk heavy cream and sugar together in a small saucepan over medium heat. Heat until the edges of the cream show fine bubbles but mixture does not boil, allowing sugar to dissolve. Remove from heat.

Step 2

Whisk butter, chocolate chips, and Irish cream into cream mixture until butter and chocolate chips are melted. Cool to room temperature.

Step 3

Scoop up the chocolate mixture about 1 tablespoon at a time and roll into a 1-inch ball; set truffles on a plate.

Step 4

Refrigerate until firm, about 1 hour.

Cook's note:

Whip the chocolate mixture to create a lighter truffle.

Nutrition Facts

Per Serving:

152 calories; protein 1g 2% DV; carbohydrates 14.6g 5% DV; fat 11.3g 17% DV; cholesterol 18.7mg 6% DV; sodium 19.5mg 1% DV.

Italian Capezzoli di Venere (Chocolate Truffles of Venus)

Prep: 1 hr 30 mins **Additional:** 30 mins **Total:** 2 hrs

Servings: 60

Yield: 60 truffles

Ingredients

- 12 ounces high quality dark chocolate, chopped
- 16 ounces canned whole chestnuts, drained
- 6 tablespoons butter, softened
- ½ cup white sugar
- ¼ cup brandy
- 1 teaspoon vanilla extract
- 12 ounces high quality white chocolate, chopped - divided
- 1 dash powdered red food coloring

Directions

Step 1

Place the dark chocolate into the top part of a double boiler over simmering water, and let the chocolate melt. Turn off the heat and let the chocolate cool.

Step 2

Place the chestnuts into the work bowl of a food processor, and process until the chestnuts are smoothly pureed, about 1 minute.

Step 3

Beat together the butter and sugar with an electric mixer until the mixture is light and fluffy, about 3 minutes. Stir in the chestnuts, brandy, and vanilla extract until the mixture is smooth. Stir in the chocolate, and pinch off about 1 tablespoon of filling per truffle. Roll the mixture into balls about 1 inch in diameter. If the mixture is too soft to hold its shape, chill for several minutes in refrigerator.

Step 4

Reserve about 1 ounce of white chocolate for tempering, and about 1 ounce for coloring. Melt the remaining 10 ounces of white chocolate over simmering water in a double boiler until the chocolate is melted and warm but not hot (about 105 degrees F (40 degrees C)). Remove the pan containing the melted chocolate from the double boiler, and add about 1 ounce of chopped, unmelted white chocolate. Stir the chocolate until the unmelted pieces of chocolate melt, and the temperature drops to 80 to 82 degrees F (27 to 28 degrees C)).

Step 5

Carefully dip each center in the melted white chocolate, and gently place the truffle onto a piece of parchment paper or waxed paper to cool and harden, about 15 minutes.

Step 6

Melt the remaining 1 ounce of chopped white chocolate over simmering water in a double boiler until the chocolate is melted and warm but not hot. Stir in a very small amount of powdered red food coloring until you get a desired shade of pink. Dip a little colored chocolate out with a spoon, dot each truffle with a pink dot, and allow the pink chocolate dots to set, about 15 minutes. Place the truffles into paper candy cups to serve.

Cook's Notes

If the filling is too thin, as it often is for me, I make the "balls" and put them in the freezer to set. In fact, I find the very solid and cold ganache is ideal for coating with chocolate, although the constant dipping of frozen centers into the hot tempered chocolate may require you to reheat the chocolate once more or maybe even twice more during the process.

If the center is too thick, thin it out, teaspoon by teaspoon, with brandy.

Nutrition Facts

Per Serving:

99 calories; protein 0.9g 2% DV; carbohydrates 12.4g 4% DV; fat 5g 8% DV; cholesterol 4.5mg 2% DV; sodium 13.7mg 1% DV.

Sweet Sierra Truffles

Prep: 30 mins **Additional:** 1 hr **Total:** 1 hr 30 mins

Servings: 200

Yield: 200 truffles

Ingredients

- 6 cups semisweet chocolate chips
- 2 (8 ounce) packages cream cheese, room temperature
- 6 cups confectioners' sugar
- 1 tablespoon sweet red wine

Directions

Step 1

Melt semisweet chocolate in a heatproof bowl set over a pan of barely simmering water. If you want to decorate with chocolate, reserve 1/2 cup of chocolate chips. Stir occasionally until melted and smooth. Remove from the heat.

Step 2

In a large bowl, beat cream cheese with an electric mixer until soft and fluffy. Gradually mix in the confectioners' sugar until completely incorporated. Stir in the melted chocolate and wine. Cover and refrigerate the dough for 1 hour, or until firm.

Step 3

Shape the mixture into 3/4 inch balls and place on a baking tray lined with waxed paper. Melt reserved chocolate chips in a small bowl in the microwave until you can stir it smooth. Use a fork to drizzle chocolate over the truffles for decoration.

Nutrition Facts

Per Serving:

47 calories; protein 0.4g 1% DV; carbohydrates 7g 2% DV; fat 2.3g 4% DV; cholesterol 2.5mg 1% DV; sodium 7.2mg.

Homemade Chocolate Covered Cherries

Servings: 50

Yield: 50 servings

Ingredients

- 8 tablespoons melted butter
- 6 tablespoons corn syrup
- 1 (14 ounce) can sweetened condensed milk
- 1 teaspoon vanilla extract

- 3 pounds confectioners' sugar
- 3 (10 ounce) jars maraschino cherries, drained
- 2 cups semisweet chocolate chips
- ½ tablespoon shortening

Directions

Step 1

In a large mixing bowl, combine butter, corn syrup, sweetened condensed milk, vanilla, and sugar. Knead dough, and form it into balls with a cherry wrapped in the middle. The balls should be approximately the size of walnuts. Place balls in the freezer to chill.

Step 2

In a double boiler, melt chocolate chips and shortening together. Dip the cooled balls in the chocolate, let cool on parchment paper.

Nutrition Facts

Per Serving:

209 calories; protein 1.2g 2% DV; carbohydrates 42.4g 14% DV; fat 4.7g 7% DV; cholesterol 7.6mg 3% DV; sodium 23.5mg 1% DV.

Peanut Butter and Banana Chocolate Truffles

Prep: 15 mins **Cook:** 5 mins **Additional:** 3 hrs 30 mins **Total:** 3 hrs 50 mins

Servings: 24

Yield: 2 dozen

Ingredients

- 12 ounces semisweet chocolate
- 1 banana, mashed
- ⅓ cup heavy whipping cream
- 2 tablespoons peanut butter
- ¼ cup sifted confectioners' sugar, or as needed

Directions

Step 1

Mix chocolate, banana, cream, and peanut butter together in a saucepan over medium heat; cook and stir mixture until melted (it may be partially lumpy due to peanut butter), 5 to 10 minutes. Pour mixture into a bowl and refrigerate until firm, 2 1/2 to 3 hours.

Step 2

Scoop chocolate mixture with a melon baller and roll into 1-inch balls. Place confectioners' sugar in a shallow bowl; coat truffles with confectioners' sugar and refrigerate until firm, 1 to 2 more hours.

Nutrition Facts

Per Serving:

99 calories; protein 1.5g 3% DV; carbohydrates 10.8g 4% DV; fat 6.4g 10% DV; cholesterol 4.5mg 2% DV; sodium 7.5mg.

Snowflake Truffles

Prep: 5 mins **Cook:** 5 mins **Additional:** 20 mins **Total:** 30 mins

Servings: 16

Yield: 16 truffles

Ingredients

- 1 ⅓ cups shredded coconut
- ½ cup confectioners' sugar
- 3 ½ ounces ricotta cheese
- 16 almonds whole almonds
- 2 ½ (1 ounce) squares white chocolate
- 2 ⅔ tablespoons heavy cream
- ¼ cup shredded coconut

Directions

Step 1

In a medium bowl, mix together 1 1/3 cups shredded coconut, sugar, and ricotta cheese to form a dough-like texture. Divide into 16 portions. Roll each portion into a ball, pressing one almond each into the center of each; cool in freezer for 20 minutes.

Step 2

Place the white chocolate in a large stainless steel bowl and set over a saucepan of barely simmering water to melt. While the chocolate is melting, stir in the heavy cream. Use a toothpick or fork to dip the truffles in the chocolate mixture. Arrange coated truffles on a platter. Sprinkle 1/4 cup coconut over the truffles while the chocolate is still melted. Cool in refrigerator until the chocolate coating solidifies.

Nutrition Facts

Per Serving:

96 calories; protein 1.5g 3% DV; carbohydrates 10.9g 4% DV; fat 5.5g 8% DV; cholesterol 6.2mg 2% DV; sodium 33.6mg 1% DV.

Rocky Road Popcorn Truffles

Prep: 30 mins **Cook:** 2 mins **Total:** 32 mins

Servings: 12

Yield: 12 candies

Ingredients

- 1 cup plain popped popcorn
- 1 cup mini marshmallows
- 1 cup salted peanuts
- 1 pound semi-sweet chocolate, chopped

Directions

Step 1

Coat a 12 cup mini muffin pan with cooking spray. Divide popcorn, marshmallows and peanuts evenly among the cups.

Step 2

Place the chocolate into a microwave-safe container. Heat on high for 45 seconds, then continue to heat at 15 second intervals, stirring each time, until chocolate is melted and smooth. Pour into the muffin cups, filling to the top. Gently tap the pan on the counter to release any bubbles. Refrigerate until chocolate is set. Unmold and enjoy!

Nutrition Facts

Per Serving:

275 calories; protein 5.6g 11% DV; carbohydrates 27.9g 9% DV; fat 18.1g 28% DV; cholesterolmg; sodium 104.2mg 4% DV.

Easy Peppermint Marshmallows

Prep: 20 mins **Cook:** 15 mins **Additional:** 4 hrs **Total:** 4 hrs 35 mins

Servings: 18

Yield: 18 marshmallows

Ingredients

- 1 serving cooking spray
- 6 tablespoons warm water
- 2 envelopes unflavored gelatin
- 1 ⅓ cups white sugar
- ½ cup light corn syrup, plus
- 2 tablespoons light corn syrup
- ¼ cup water
- ¼ teaspoon salt
- 1 ½ teaspoons vanilla extract
- ¾ teaspoon pure peppermint extract

- red food coloring
- ¼ cup cornstarch

- ¼ cup confectioners' sugar

Directions

Step 1

Line a 9x9 pan with plastic wrap, leaving enough overhang to cover the top. Spray plastic wrap lightly with cooking spray. Place the 6 tablespoons of warm water in a large bowl, and sprinkle gelatin on top. Let gelatin soften in the water for 5 minutes.

Step 2

Combine the white sugar, corn syrup, and 1/4 cup water in a tall saucepan. Bring to a boil, stirring constantly. Boil for one full minute, 240 degrees F on a candy thermometer. Pour the hot syrup over the softened gelatin, and add the salt. Beat at high speed with an electric mixer until the mixture increases in volume and holds a peak, about 8 to 10 minutes. Stir in the vanilla and peppermint extracts.

Step 3

Pour into prepared pan, add several drops of red food coloring, and swirl with a toothpick. Cover lightly with plastic wrap, and let stand at room temperature for 4 hours. Cut into 18 squares, using a knife sprayed with cooking spray. Combine cornstarch and powdered sugar in a bowl. Toss cut marshmallows in the reserved powdered sugar mixture. Store in airtight container or resealable plastic bag.

Nutrition Facts

Per Serving:

107 calories; protein 0.7g 1% DV; carbohydrates 26.9g 9% DV; fatg; cholesterolmg; sodium 41.6mg 2% DV.

Cherry Chocolate Bark

Prep: 5 mins **Cook:** 5 mins **Additional:** 30 mins **Total:** 40 mins

Servings: 18

Yield: 18 ounces

Ingredients

- 1 (12 ounce) bag semisweet chocolate chips
- 12 eaches cherry-flavored candy canes, crushed
- ⅓ cup red confectioner's coating

Directions

Step 1

Line a 9x13 inch baking pan with aluminum foil.

Step 2

Melt the chocolate chips in a microwave-safe glass or ceramic bowl in 30-second intervals, stirring after each melting, until smooth, 1 to 3 minutes (depending on your microwave). Do not overheat or chocolate will scorch. Using a spatula, quickly spread the melted chocolate evenly in the prepared pan until the bottom of the pan is covered. Sprinkle the crushed candy evenly over the chocolate, and pat lightly with a clean spatula to help the candy settle into the chocolate.

Step 3

Melt the red confectioner's coating, if using, in a microwave-safe glass or ceramic bowl in 30-second intervals, stirring after each melting, until smooth, 1 to 3 minutes (depending on your microwave). Spoon the melted coating into a resealable plastic bag; snip off a very small corner of the bag, and use to drizzle coating over the bark.

Step 4

Place the pan in the refrigerator or freezer until hardened, about 30 minutes. Remove from pan; peel off foil. Break into small pieces to serve.

Cook's Note

Crushing candy canes is easy when placed in a resealable plastic bag and smashed with a hammer on top of a sturdy wooden or plastic cutting board. The bag will tear a little, but does not interfere with crushing.

Nutrition Facts

Per Serving:

180 calories; protein 1g 2% DV; carbohydrates 31.9g 10% DV; fat 6.6g 10% DV; cholesterol 0.7mg; sodium 12mg 1% DV.

Valentin's Day Cookie

Easy Valentine Sandwich Cookies

Servings: 17

Yield: 34 cookies

Ingredients

- 1 cup butter
- 1 ½ cups confectioners' sugar
- 1 egg
- 1 teaspoon vanilla extract
- ½ teaspoon almond extract
- 2 ½ cups all-purpose flour
- 1 teaspoon baking soda
- 1 teaspoon cream of tartar

Directions

Step 1

In a large bowl, cream together butter and confectioners' sugar. Beat in egg, vanilla and almond extract. Mix well.

Step 2

In a medium bowl, stir together flour, baking soda and cream of tartar; blend into the butter mixture. Divide dough into thirds and shape into balls.

Step 3

Working with 1/3 of dough at a time, roll out dough into desired thickness on a lightly floured surface. For each heart sandwich cookie, cut out 2 3-inch hearts. Cut out the center of ONE of the 3-inch hearts with the 1 1/2-inch cutter.

Step 4

Place each piece separately on an ungreased cookie sheet, 1 - 2 inches apart. Bake in a preheated, 350 degrees F (175 degrees C) oven until lightly browned (7-8 minutes for 1/4 inch thick cookies). Cool completely on wire rack. Frost bottom cookie with Pink Valentine Frosting and place an open centered cookie on top to form the sandwich. Also frost the small 1 1/2 inch hearts and serve as separate cookies.

Nutrition Facts

Per Serving:

210 calories; protein 2.4g 5% DV; carbohydrates 24.7g 8% DV; fat 11.3g 17% DV; cholesterol 39.7mg 13% DV; sodium 155.7mg 6% DV.

Plum Jam Cookies

Servings: 24

Yield: 4 dozen

Ingredients

- 8 ounces butter
- 1 cup packed brown sugar
- 1 egg
- 1 teaspoon baking soda
- ¼ cup water
- 3 cups all-purpose flour
- 1 pinch salt
- 1 teaspoon baking powder
- 1 cup plum preserves

Directions

Step 1

Preheat oven to 375 degrees F(190 degrees C).

Step 2

In a large bowl, cream together the butter and brown sugar. Beat in the egg and water. Sift together the flour, baking powder, and salt; stir into the butter mixture until well blended.

Step 3

On a lightly floured surface, roll out the dough to 1/4 inch thickness. Cut with a 2 inch round cookie cutter. Put half of the cookies onto a cookie sheet and spread 1/2 of a teaspoon of plum jam in the center of each one. With a thimble, or small cookie cutter , cut the center out of the remaining cookies. Place these on top of the jam topped cookies to make sandwiches. Press together. Bake cookies for 10 minutes then remove to a rack to cool.

Nutrition Facts

Per Serving:

197 calories; protein 2g 4% DV; carbohydrates 30.2g 10% DV; fat 7.9g 12% DV; cholesterol 27.8mg 9% DV; sodium 132.3mg 5% DV.

Easy Red Velvet Sandwich Cookies

Prep: 25 mins **Cook:** 8 mins **Total:** 33 mins

Servings: 24

Yield: 24 cookies

Ingredients

- 1 (18.25 ounce) box red velvet cake mix
- 2 eaches eggs, lightly beaten
- ½ cup vegetable oil
- 1 tablespoon bourbon

Icing

- 1 (8 ounce) package cream cheese, softened
- ¼ cup butter, softened
- 2 teaspoons evaporated milk
- 1 teaspoon vanilla
- ½ cup flaked coconut
- 4 cups confectioners' sugar
- ½ cup chopped pecans

Directions

Step 1

Preheat the oven to 375 degrees F (190 degrees C).

Step 2

Mix together cake mix, eggs, oil, and bourbon in a large bowl. Roll the dough into balls the size of walnuts. Place 2 inches apart on ungreased baking sheets.

Step 3

Bake in the preheated oven until the tops start to crack, about 8 minutes. Cool in the pans for 10 minutes before removing to cool completely on a wire rack.

Step 4

In a large bowl combine cream cheese, butter, evaporated milk, vanilla, and coconut. Add the confectioners' sugar 1 cup at a time, mixing well with each addition. If consistency is too stiff, add more milk.

Step 5

Place the chopped pecans in a bowl. Spread a generous amount of icing on the bottom of a cookie, sandwich it with another cookie, pressing firmly so that the icing comes all the way out to the edge. Roll the edges of the sandwich cookies in the chopped pecans. Repeat with the remaining cookies.

Nutrition Facts

Per Serving:

292 calories; protein 2.5g 5% DV; carbohydrates 39.9g 13% DV; fat 14.3g 22% DV; cholesterol 29.1mg 10% DV; sodium 182.1mg 7% DV.

Heart Cookies Decorated with Royal Icing

Prep: 1 hr **Cook:** 10 mins **Additional:** 2 hrs 15 mins **Total:** 3 hrs 25 mins

Servings: 24

Yield: 24 cookies

Ingredients

- 1 cup unsalted butter, softened
- 2 tablespoons unsalted butter, softened
- 1 ¼ cups white sugar
- 1 tablespoon lemon zest
- 2 large eggs eggs
- 2 cups all-purpose flour, sifted
- Royal Icing:
- 2 large egg whites egg whites
- 3 cups sifted confectioners' sugar
- 1 teaspoon lemon juice, or as needed
- red food coloring

Directions

Step 1

Cream 1 cup plus 2 tablespoons butter in a large bowl with an electric mixer. Add white sugar and lemon zest and mix well. Mix in eggs one at a time and beat well after each addition. Mix in 1/2 of the flour until combined. Mix in remaining flour until dough comes together.

Step 2

Shape dough with your hands into a thick rectangle. Press flat and wrap in plastic wrap. Refrigerate for 2 hours.

Step 3

Preheat the oven to 350 degrees F (175 degrees C). Line 2 baking sheets with parchment paper.

Step 4

Dust a work surface with flour and roll out dough into a thin circle. Cut out heart shapes and arrange cut-out cookies on the prepared baking sheets.

Step 5

Bake in the preheated oven until lightly browned, 10 to 15 minutes. Remove hearts from baking sheets carefully and transfer to wire racks. Cool completely, about 15 minutes.

Step 6

Beat egg whites in a bowl until frothy. Beat in confectioners' sugar, 1 tablespoon at a time, until stiff peaks form. Add lemon juice to thin out the mixture. Add more lemon juice for runnier icing. Divide icing into small bowls and color with red food coloring in different shades of red or pink, keeping a portion of the icing white. Cover with a damp kitchen towel at all times so it won't dry out.

Step 7

Decorate as you like using different techniques. For the flood technique, use runny royal icing in a piping bag with a small round #2 tip and pipe a line around the edge of the cookies. Fill in the center, evenly distributing the icing with a scriber tool.

Step 8

For hearts, add dots of a different color onto the wet icing and drag the scriber tool downwards through the dots. For lips, add an oval shape onto the wet icing and shape the oval into lips with the scriber tool.

Step 9

For feathers or patterns, pipe a line around the edge, then add stripes in different colors. Drag the scriber tool down through the stripes. For a marbled effect, pipe lines of different colors across a base layer, then drag the scriber tool up and down through the lines. Allow the icing to set completely.

Cook's Note:

Baking time is often shorter after the first batch of cookies.

Nutrition Facts

Per Serving:

223 calories; protein 2g 4% DV; carbohydrates 34.1g 11% DV; fat 9.2g 14% DV; cholesterol 38.4mg 13% DV; sodium 12mg 1% DV.

German Heart Cookies

Prep: 45 mins **Cook:** 10 mins **Additional:** 4 hrs 20 mins **Total:** 5 hrs 15 mins

Servings: 50

Yield: 50 cookies

Ingredients

- 3 ¼ cups all-purpose flour
- 1 cup unsalted butter
- 2 tablespoons unsalted butter

- 1 cup white sugar
- 2 eaches eggs

Icing:

- 2 cups confectioners' sugar, divided
- 1 tablespoon lemon juice, or more as needed

- 1 tablespoon raspberry syrup, or more as needed

Directions

Step 1

Combine flour, 1 cup plus 2 tablespoons butter, white sugar, and eggs in a large bowl and knead into a smooth dough. Shape into a ball. Flatten, cover with plastic wrap, and refrigerate for 2 hours.

Step 2

Preheat oven to 375 degrees F (190 degrees C). Grease 2 baking sheets or line with parchment paper.

Step 3

Dust a work surface with flour and roll out dough to 1/4-inch thickness. Cut out hearts with a heart-shaped cookie cutter and arrange cut-out cookies on prepared baking sheets.

Step 4

Bake in the preheated oven until lightly browned, 10 to 15 minutes. Remove from baking sheets carefully and transfer to wire racks. Cool completely, about 20 minutes.

Step 5

Mix 1 cup of confectioners' sugar with as much lemon juice needed to form a thick icing. Cover half of the hearts with the white icing. Mix the remaining 1 cup confectioners' sugar with raspberry syrup and cover the other half with pink icing. Let cookies stand until icing dries completely, about 2 hours, or up to overnight.

Nutrition Facts

Per Serving:

105 calories; protein 1.1g 2% DV; carbohydrates 15.5g 5% DV; fat 4.4g 7% DV; cholesterol 17.5mg 6% DV; sodium 3.2mg.

Valentine Cookies

Servings: 12

Yield: 2 dozen

Ingredients

- ½ pound butter, softened
- 2 ½ cups sifted all-purpose flour
- 1 cup sifted confectioners' sugar
- 1 tablespoon milk
- 1 teaspoon vanilla extract

Directions

Step 1

Preheat oven to 325 degrees F (170 degrees C).

Step 2

Mix butter in a mixer until light, add remaining ingredients.

Step 3

Knead until velvety. Roll one-half of the dough at a time to about 1/4 inch thickness using the smallest amount of flour possible.

Step 4

Cut out and bake on a lightly greased pan for 12 minutes. Cookies will be almost white when cooked.

Nutrition Facts

Per Serving:

273 calories; protein 2.9g 6% DV; carbohydrates 30.4g 10% DV; fat 15.6g 24% DV; cholesterol 40.8mg 14% DV; sodium 110.1mg 4% DV.

Valentine Heart Necklaces

Prep: 35 mins **Cook:** 7 mins **Additional:** 2 hrs **Total:** 2 hrs 42 mins

Servings: 15

Yield: 30 cookies

Ingredients

- 1 cup butter, softened
- ¾ cup white sugar
- 1 egg
- 1 teaspoon vanilla extract
- 1 tablespoon lemon zest
- 2 ½ cups sifted all-purpose flour
- 1 teaspoon baking powder
- 3 cups confectioners' sugar
- ⅓ cup butter, softened
- 1 ½ teaspoons vanilla extract
- 2 tablespoons milk
- 3 drops red food coloring
- 2 ¼ ounces colored candy sprinkles
- 60 piece (blank)s long red vine licorice

Directions

Step 1

Cream 1 cup butter or margarine and 3/4 cup white sugar together. Blend in egg, 1 teaspoon vanilla extract, and grated lemon peel. Sift together 2 1/2 cups all-purpose flour and baking powder. Add to creamed mixture and blend well. Cover and refrigerate dough for approximately 2 hours.

Step 2

Preheat oven to 375 degrees F (190 degrees C).

Step 3

Roll dough to 1/4 inch thickness on a lightly floured surface. Use a floured heart shaped 1 to 2 inch cookie cutter and cut dough into heart shapes. Place the cut-out hearts on greased cookie sheets.

Step 4

Using the drinking straw, make a hole at the top center of each heart before baking. Bake for 5 to 7 minutes until very lightly browned. Cool the cookies on a wire rack.

Step 5

To Make Butter Frosting: Mix 3 cups confectioners' sugar and 1/3 cup butter together. Stir in 1 1/2 teaspoons vanilla extract and 2 tablespoons milk. Beat until smooth making sure frosting is of spreading consistency. Stir in food coloring to create a pink or red colored frosting, if desired.

Step 6

After cookies have cooled, frost and decorate them with nonpareils, sprinkles, dragees, or colored sugar. Use a toothpick to dislodge the hole, if necessary. Let the frosting dry.

Step 7

To make a necklace, tie the ends off of two pieces of red colored licorice with a knot. Thread it through the hole at the top center of the cookie. Tie the other ends off with another knot to create a "chain." Makes approximately 30 heart necklaces.

Nutrition Facts

Per Serving:

521 calories; protein 3.9g 8% DV; carbohydrates 87.2g 28% DV; fat 17.8g 27% DV; cholesterol 56mg 19% DV; sodium 175.6mg 7% DV.

Chili Chocolate Cookies

Prep: 20 mins **Cook:** 15 mins **Additional:** 10 mins **Total:** 45 mins

Servings: 12

Yield: 24 Cookies

Ingredients

- ½ cup dried currants
- 2 tablespoons coffee flavored liqueur (such as Kahlua)
- 4 ounces unsweetened chocolate
- 2 ounces bittersweet chocolate
- 3 tablespoons unsalted butter
- ½ cup all-purpose flour
- ½ teaspoon freshly ground black pepper
- ¼ teaspoon baking powder
- ¼ teaspoon salt
- ⅛ teaspoon ground cinnamon
- ⅛ teaspoon cayenne pepper
- ¾ cup sugar
- 2 medium (blank)s eggs
- 2 teaspoons vanilla extract
- 1 cup dark chocolate chips

Directions

Step 1

Preheat oven to 350 degrees F (175 degrees C).

Step 2

Line two baking sheets with parchment paper or silicone baking mats.

Step 3

Heat currants and coffee liqueur in a saucepan over low heat until it begins to simmer, about 2 minutes. Remove from heat and set aside.

Step 4

Combine unsweetened chocolate, bittersweet chocolate, and butter in bowl. Place bowl on top of a saucepan filled with 1-inch of water set over low heat. Stir chocolate mixture occasionally until melted, about 5 minutes. Remove from heat and set aside.

Step 5

Mix flour, black pepper, baking powder, salt, cinnamon, and cayenne pepper in large bowl and set aside.

Step 6

Whisk sugar and eggs in a small bowl until light, fluffy, and pale yellow, about 5 minutes. Slowly whisk in vanilla and melted chocolate mixture.

Step 7

Fold flour mixture into sugar and chocolate mixture until combined.

Step 8

Stir in dark chocolate chips and liqueur-soaked currants.

Step 9

Drop spoonfuls of cookie dough 2 inches apart onto prepared baking sheets.

Step 10

Bake in the preheated oven until cookies are almost set, about 12 minutes.

Step 11

Remove from the oven and leave on baking sheets to cool, 5 minutes.

Step 12

Transfer to cooling rack and allow to finish cooling, 5 minutes.

Nutrition Facts

Per Serving:

272 calories; protein 3.9g 8% DV; carbohydrates 36.4g 12% DV; fat 14.3g 22% DV; cholesterol 35.1mg 12% DV; sodium 74.2mg 3% DV.

Lollipop Cookie Valentines

Servings: 6

Yield: 1 dozen

Ingredients

- 12 eaches craft sticks
- ½ cup semisweet chocolate chips
- ½ cup butter, softened
- ⅓ cup packed light brown sugar
- ½ teaspoon vanilla extract
- 1 egg
- 2 cups all-purpose flour
- ¼ cup unsweetened cocoa powder
- ¼ teaspoon salt
- 12 (1 ounce) squares white chocolate
- 1 egg white
- 1 ¼ cups confectioners' sugar
- 3 drops red food coloring

Directions

Step 1

Soak craft sticks for one hour in a bowl of cold water.

Step 2

In small heavy saucepan over very low heat, stir chocolate chips until melted and smooth. Remove from heat; let cool.

Step 3

In large bowl with electric mixer at medium speed, beat butter, brown sugar and vanilla until fluffy. Beat egg in well; beat in cooled chocolate. With mixer at low speed, beat in flour, cocoa powder and salt until smooth. Divide dough in half.

Step 4

Preheat oven to 375 degrees F (190 degrees C) and grease 2 large cookie sheets.

Step 5

Roll each half out to 1/8 inch thickness between 2 sheets of wax paper; freeze, in wax paper, 5 minutes. Peal top sheets of wax paper off dough; cut dough out using 3-inch heart-shaped cutter. Reroll scraps; freeze again 5 minutes; cut out. Place half of the hearts 1 inch apart on prepared cookie sheet.

Step 6

Drain sticks, pat dry. Place one stick on each heart to make 2 1/2 inch handle, pressing lightly into dough. Place remaining hearts on top; press edges gently to seal. Bake about 12 minutes until firm to touch. Cool on wire racks.

Step 7

In 2-quart heavy saucepan over very low heat, or in top of double boiler set over barely simmering water, stir white or milk chocolate until melted and smooth; if using both chocolates, melt in separate 1-quart pans. Remove from heat.

Step 8

Holding each lollipop by handle, dip into chocolate to coat on both sides; let excess chocolate drip back into pan. Place each lollipop as it is coated on wax-paper-lined cookie sheet; refrigerate 20 minutes until chocolate is set.

Step 9

To Make Icing: In large bowl with electric mixer at high speed, beat egg white and confectioners' sugar until very smooth. If desired, remove small portion of icing to separate bowl; tint with drops of food coloring. Spoon icing into decorating bag fitted with small writing tip; pipe over lollipops in desired patterns. Decorate with assorted candies and decors; attaching with dots of icing.

Nutrition Facts

Per Serving:

838 calories; protein 11.3g 23% DV; carbohydrates 111.2g 36% DV; fat 41g 63% DV; cholesterol 83.5mg 28% DV; sodium 292.8mg 12% DV.

Sugar Cookie Icing

Prep: 15 mins **Total:** 15 mins

Servings: 12

Yield: 1 dozen cookies' worth

Ingredients

- 1 cup confectioners' sugar
- 2 teaspoons milk
- 2 teaspoons light corn syrup
- ¼ teaspoon almond extract

Recommended:

- assorted food coloring

Directions

Step 1

In a small bowl, stir together confectioners' sugar and milk until smooth. Beat in corn syrup and almond extract until icing is smooth and glossy. If icing is too thick, add more corn syrup.

Step 2

Divide into separate bowls, and add food colorings to each to desired intensity. Dip cookies, or paint them with a brush.

Nutrition Facts

Per Serving:

42 calories; proteing; carbohydrates 10.8g 4% DV; fatg; cholesterolmg; sodium 0.8mg.

The Best Rolled Sugar Cookies

Prep: 20 mins **Cook:** 8 mins **Additional:** 2 hrs 32 mins **Total:** 3 hrs

Servings: 60

Yield: 5 dozen

Ingredients

- 1 ½ cups butter, softened
- 2 cups white sugar

- 4 large eggs eggs
- 1 teaspoon vanilla extract
- 5 cups all-purpose flour
- 2 teaspoons baking powder
- 1 teaspoon salt

Directions

Step 1

In a large bowl, cream together butter and sugar until smooth. Beat in eggs and vanilla. Stir in the flour, baking powder, and salt. Cover, and chill dough for at least one hour (or overnight).

Step 2

Preheat oven to 400 degrees F (200 degrees C). Roll out dough on floured surface 1/4 to 1/2 inch thick. Cut into shapes with any cookie cutter. Place cookies 1 inch apart on ungreased cookie sheets.

Step 3

Bake 6 to 8 minutes in preheated oven. Cool completely.

Nutrition Facts

Per Serving:

110 calories; protein 1.5g 3% DV; carbohydrates 14.7g 5% DV; fat 5g 8% DV; cholesterol 24.6mg 8% DV; sodium 92.6mg 4% DV.

Valentine's Day Sugar Cookies

Prep: 25 mins **Cook:** 10 mins **Additional:** 20 mins **Total:** 55 mins

Servings: 24

Yield: 2 dozen medium cookies

Ingredients

- 1 cup butter, softened
- 1 cup white sugar
- 1 egg
- 1 teaspoon vanilla extract
- ½ teaspoon almond extract
- 3 cups all-purpose flour
- 2 teaspoons baking powder
- ½ (16 ounce) package white confectioners' coating (such as CANDIQUIK), or as needed
- 1 (3 ounce) bar red candy melts (such as Wilton), or as needed

Directions

Step 1

Preheat the oven to 350 degrees F (175 degrees C).

Step 2

Beat butter and sugar together in the bowl of a stand mixer fitted with a paddle attachment until smooth. Beat in egg, vanilla, and almond extract.

Step 3

Combine flour and baking powder in a separate bowl and add to the butter mixture, a little at a time. Stir until well combined. Knead using wet fingers if dough gets too stiff, dusting with flouring occasionally, until it bounces back.

Step 4

Roll dough out to uniform thinness and cut into desired shapes. Place 2 inches apart onto cookie sheets.

Step 5

Bake in the preheated oven until edges are golden, about 10 minutes. Cool on the cookie sheets until firm enough to transfer to a cooling rack.

Step 6

Meanwhile, melt confectioners' coating in the microwave according to manufacturer's instructions. Mix in red candy melts until desired color is reached. Dip cooled cookies in the candy coating and let rest on waxed paper until hardened, about 5 minutes.

Cook's Note:

If you cannot find something comparable to red (or pink) candy melts, buy an oil-based food coloring.

Nutrition Facts

Per Serving:

231 calories; protein 2.7g 5% DV; carbohydrates 28.1g 9% DV; fat 12.2g 19% DV; cholesterol 30.8mg 10% DV; sodium 110.1mg 4% DV.

Cream Cheese Sugar Cookies

Prep: 15 mins **Cook:** 10 mins **Additional:** 9 hrs **Total:** 9 hrs 25 mins

Servings: 72

Yield: 6 dozen

Ingredients

- 1 cup white sugar
- 1 cup butter, softened
- 1 (3 ounce) package cream cheese, softened
- ½ teaspoon salt
- ½ teaspoon almond extract
- ½ teaspoon vanilla extract
- 1 egg yolk
- 2 ¼ cups all-purpose flour

Directions

Step 1

In a large bowl, combine the sugar, butter, cream cheese, salt, almond and vanilla extracts, and egg yolk. Beat until smooth. Stir in flour until well blended. Chill the dough for 8 hours, or overnight.

Step 2

Preheat oven to 375 degrees F (190 degrees C).

Step 3

On a lightly floured surface, roll out the dough 1/3 at a time to 1/8 inch thickness, refrigerating remaining dough until ready to use. Cut into desired shapes with lightly floured cookie cutters. Place 1 inch apart on ungreased cookie sheets. Leave cookies plain for frosting, or brush with slightly beaten egg white and sprinkle with candy sprinkles or colored sugar.

Step 4

Bake for 7 to 10 minutes in the preheated oven, or until light and golden brown. Cool cookies completely before frosting.

Nutrition Facts

Per Serving:

53 calories; protein 0.6g 1% DV; carbohydrates 5.8g 2% DV; fat 3.1g 5% DV; cholesterol 10.9mg 4% DV; sodium 38mg 2% DV.

Chocolate Truffle Cookies

Prep: 15 mins **Cook:** 10 mins **Additional:** 1 hr 35 mins **Total:** 2 hrs

Servings: 36

Yield: 3 dozen

Ingredients

- 4 (1 ounce) squares unsweetened chocolate, chopped
- 1 cup semisweet chocolate chips
- 6 tablespoons butter
- 3 large eggs eggs
- 1 cup white sugar
- 1 ½ teaspoons vanilla extract
- ½ cup all-purpose flour
- 2 tablespoons unsweetened cocoa powder
- ¼ teaspoon baking powder
- ¼ teaspoon salt
- 1 cup semisweet chocolate chips

Directions

Step 1

In the microwave or in a metal bowl over a pan of simmering water, melt unsweetened chocolate, 1 cup of the chocolate chips, and the butter stirring occasionally until smooth. Remove from heat and set aside to cool. In a large bowl, whip eggs and sugar until thick and pale, about 2 minutes. Stir in the vanilla and the chocolate mixture until well mixed. Combine the flour, cocoa, baking powder and salt; gradually stir into the chocolate mixture. Fold in remaining 1 cup chocolate chips. Cover dough and chill for at least an hour or overnight.

Step 2

Preheat oven to 350 degrees F (175 degrees C). Roll chilled dough into 1 inch balls. Place on ungreased cookie sheets so they are 2 inches apart.

Step 3

Bake for 9 to 11 minutes in the preheated oven. Allow cookies to cool on baking sheet for 5 minutes before removing to a wire rack to cool completely.

Nutrition Facts

Per Serving:

112 calories; protein 1.6g 3% DV; carbohydrates 13.9g 5% DV; fat 6.8g 11% DV; cholesterol 20.6mg 7% DV; sodium 40mg 2% DV.

Ultimate Double Chocolate Cookies

Prep: 25 mins **Cook:** 10 mins **Additional:** 1 hr 5 mins **Total:** 1 hr 40 mins

Servings: 42

Yield: 3 1/2 dozen

Ingredients

- 1 pound semisweet chocolate, chopped
- 2 cups all-purpose flour
- ½ cup Dutch process cocoa powder
- 2 teaspoons baking powder
- 1 teaspoon salt
- 10 tablespoons unsalted butter
- 1 ½ cups packed brown sugar
- ½ cup white sugar
- 4 large eggs eggs
- 2 teaspoons instant coffee granules
- 2 teaspoons vanilla extract

Directions

Step 1

Melt chocolate over a double boiler or in the microwave, stirring occasionally until smooth. Sift together flour, cocoa, baking powder, and salt; set aside.

Step 2

In a medium bowl, cream butter with white sugar and brown sugar until smooth. Beat in eggs one at a time, then stir in coffee crystals and vanilla until well blended. Stir in melted chocolate. Using a wooden spoon, stir in the dry ingredients just until everything comes together. Cover, and let stand for 35 minutes so the chocolate can set up.

Step 3

Preheat the oven to 350 degrees F (175 degrees C). Line two cookie sheets with parchment paper. Roll dough into walnut sized balls, or drop by rounded tablespoonfuls onto the prepared cookie sheets, leaving 2 inches between cookies.

Step 4

Bake for 8 to 10 minutes in the preheated oven. Cookies will be set, but the centers will still be very soft because of the chocolate. Allow cookies to cool on the baking sheets for 10 minutes before transferring to wire racks to cool completely.

Nutrition Facts

Soft Sugar Cookies

Servings: 24

Yield: 4 1/2 dozen

Ingredients

- ⅔ cup shortening
- ⅔ cup butter
- 1 ½ cups white sugar
- 2 large eggs eggs
- 2 teaspoons vanilla extract
- 3 ½ cups all-purpose flour
- 2 teaspoons baking powder
- 1 teaspoon salt
- ⅓ cup granulated sugar for decoration

Directions

Step 1

Preheat oven to 350 degrees F (175 degrees C).

Step 2

In a medium bowl, cream together the butter, shortening and sugar. Stir in the eggs and vanilla. Combine the flour, baking powder and salt, stir into the creamed mixture until dough comes together. Roll dough into walnut sized balls and roll the balls in sugar. Place them on an unprepared cookie sheet about 2 inches apart.

Step 3

Bake cookies 10 to 12 minutes in the preheated oven, until bottom is light brown. Remove from baking sheets to cool on wire racks.

Nutrition Facts

Per Serving:

228 calories; protein 2.5g 5% DV; carbohydrates 29.4g 10% DV; fat 11.4g 18% DV; cholesterol 29.1mg 10% DV; sodium 180.1mg 7% DV.

Red Velvet Cookies

Prep: 30 mins **Cook:** 10 mins **Total:** 40 mins

Servings: 36

Yield: 36 servings

Ingredients

- 2 cups all-purpose flour
- ½ teaspoon baking soda
- ½ teaspoon salt
- 2 (1 ounce) squares unsweetened baking chocolate, broken into pieces
- ½ cup unsalted butter, softened
- ⅔ cup brown sugar, firmly packed
- ⅓ cup white sugar
- 1 large egg
- 1 tablespoon red food coloring
- ¾ cup sour cream
- 1 cup semisweet chocolate chips
- Cream Cheese Frosting
- ¼ cup unsalted butter, softened
- 4 ounces cream cheese, at room temperature
- ½ teaspoon vanilla extract
- 2 cups confectioners' sugar, sifted

Directions

Step 1

Preheat oven to 375 degrees F (190 degrees C) with the rack in the middle position. Grease baking sheets or line with parchment paper. Sift together the flour, baking soda, and salt.

Step 2

Break the chocolate squares into chunks, place in a microwave-safe bowl and microwave on High until the chocolate melts, about 90 seconds. Stir the chocolate until smooth and set aside to cool.

Step 3

In a large bowl, beat 1/2 cup butter, brown sugar, and white sugar until light and fluffy; pour in the egg and beat until smooth. Mix in the red food coloring and chocolate, scraping the bowl down regularly, until evenly blended, about 30 seconds. Add half of the sifted dry ingredients, stirring until well incorporated. Beat in the sour cream and mix in the remaining dry ingredients. Fold in the chocolate chips. Drop spoonfuls of the dough 2 inches apart onto prepared baking sheets.

Step 4

Bake one sheet at a time in the preheated oven until they spring back when pressed, about 9 minutes. Cool in the pans for 5 minutes before removing to cool completely on a wire rack.

Step 5

For the cream cheese frosting, whip 1/4 cup butter, cream cheese, and vanilla until smooth. Blend in the powdered sugar in half cup portions until the frosting reaches the desired consistency.

Nutrition Facts

Per Serving:

163 calories; protein 1.7g 3% DV; carbohydrates 21.8g 7% DV; fat 8.4g 13% DV; cholesterol 20.9mg 7% DV; sodium 66.4mg 3% DV.

Butter Snow Flakes

Prep: 15 mins **Cook:** 15 mins **Additional:** 30 mins **Total:** 1 hr

Servings: 36

Yield: 6 dozen

Ingredients

- 2 ¼ cups all-purpose flour
- ¼ teaspoon salt
- ¼ teaspoon ground cinnamon
- 1 cup butter
- 1 (3 ounce) package cream cheese, softened
- 1 cup white sugar
- 1 egg yolk
- 1 teaspoon vanilla extract
- 1 teaspoon orange zest

Directions

Step 1

Preheat oven to 350 degrees F (175 degrees C). Sift together the flour, salt, and cinnamon; set aside.

Step 2

In a medium bowl, cream together butter and cream cheese. Add sugar and egg yolk; beat until light and fluffy. Stir in the vanilla and orange zest. Gradually blend in the dry ingredients. Fill a cookie press or pastry bag with dough, and form cookies on an ungreased cookie sheet.

Step 3

Bake for 12 to 15 minutes in the preheated oven, or until the cookies are golden brown on the peaks and on the bottoms. Remove from cookie sheets at once to cool on wire racks.

Boyfriend Brownies

Prep: 15 mins **Cook:** 45 mins **Additional:** 2 hrs **Total:** 3 hrs

Servings: 16

Yield: 1 9x9-inch pan

Ingredients

- 1 ½ cups all-purpose flour
- 1 teaspoon baking soda
- ½ teaspoon salt
- 1 ½ cups white sugar
- ¼ cup water
- ⅔ cup butter
- 1 (12 ounce) bag semisweet chocolate chips
- 2 teaspoons vanilla extract
- 4 large eggs eggs
- 1 (12 ounce) bag semisweet chocolate chips
- 1 cup coarsely chopped walnuts

Directions

Step 1

Preheat an oven to 325 degrees F (165 degrees C). Combine the flour, baking soda, and salt in a small bowl; set aside. Grease and flour a 9x9-inch baking dish.

Step 2

Combine the sugar, water, and butter in a saucepan. Cook and stir over medium heat until the butter has melted and the sugar has dissolved. Remove from the heat and stir in one bag of chocolate chips and the vanilla extract until the chocolate has melted. Pour the mixture into a mixing bowl, and beat in the eggs one at a time until smooth. Fold in the flour mixture until incorporated, then fold in the remaining bag of chocolate chips along with the walnuts. Pour into prepared pan.

Step 3

Bake in the preheated oven until the top is dry and the edges have started to pull away from the sides of the pan, 45 to 55 minutes. Cool completely before cutting into squares to serve.

Crispy Peanut Butter Chocolate Log

Prep: 15 mins **Cook:** 5 mins **Additional:** 1 hr **Total:** 1 hr 20 mins

Servings: 12

Ingredients

- 1 (10 ounce) package large marshmallows
- ¼ cup butter
- ¼ cup peanut butter
- 5 ½ cups crispy rice cereal (such as Rice Krispies)
- 1 ⅓ cups semi-sweet chocolate chips
- ¾ cup butterscotch chips

Directions

Step 1

Line a 15x10x1-inch pan with waxed paper. Grease the waxed paper.

Step 2

Combine marshmallows, butter, and peanut butter together in a large microwave-safe bowl. Cover bowl and heat mixture in the microwave until marshmallows are melted, about 2 minutes. Stir well.

Step 3

Stir rice cereal into marshmallow mixture until well coated; spread onto the prepared pan.

Step 4

Combine chocolate chips and butterscotch chips in a microwave-safe bowl. Heat mixture in microwave until melted, about 2 minutes. Stir well.

Step 5

Spread chocolate mixture over rice cereal mixture, leaving a 1-inch border around edges. Roll rice cereal mixture around chocolate filling, jelly-roll style and starting with the short side. Peel waxed paper away while rolling. Place roll, seam-side down, on a serving platter. Refrigerate until set, about 1 hour. Cut into narrow slices.

Nutrition Facts

Per Serving:

338 calories; protein 3.5g 7% DV; carbohydrates 50g 16% DV; fat 15.4g 24% DV; cholesterol 10.2mg 3% DV; sodium 182.2mg 7% DV.

Chocolate Chip Meringue

Servings: 24

Yield: 4 dozen

Ingredients

- 3 large egg whites egg whites
- 1 cup white sugar
- ½ teaspoon distilled white vinegar
- ½ teaspoon vanilla extract
- 1 pinch salt
- 2 cups semisweet chocolate chips

Directions

Step 1

Preheat oven to 300 degrees F (150 degrees C). Grease baking sheets or line them with parchment paper.

Step 2

In a medium bowl, whip egg whites to soft peaks. Gradually add the sugar, vinegar and vanilla while whipping to stiff peaks. Fold in chocolate chips. Drop by spoonfuls onto the prepared cookie sheets.

Step 3

Bake for 20 to 25 minutes in the preheated oven, until cookies are dry.

Nutrition Facts

Per Serving:

102 calories; protein 1g 2% DV; carbohydrates 17.2g 6% DV; fat 4.2g 7% DV; cholesterolmg; sodium 8.5mg.

Red Velvet Chocolate Chip Cookies

Prep: 20 mins **Cook:** 10 mins **Additional:** 1 hr **Total:** 1 hr 30 mins

Servings: 15

Yield: 15 cookies

Ingredients

- 1 ½ cups all-purpose flour
- ⅓ cup unsweetened cocoa powder
- 1 teaspoon baking soda
- ½ teaspoon baking powder
- ½ teaspoon salt
- ½ cup butter, softened
- ¾ cup brown sugar
- ¼ cup white sugar
- 1 egg
- 1 ½ tablespoons milk
- 1 ½ teaspoons vanilla extract
- 2 tablespoons red food coloring
- 1 cup dark chocolate chips, or as needed

Directions

Step 1

Whisk flour, cocoa powder, baking soda, baking powder, and salt together in a bowl.

Step 2

Beat butter with an electric mixer until fluffy, about 2 minutes; beat in brown sugar and white sugar until smooth, about 1 minute. Beat egg, milk, and vanilla extract into butter mixture; beat in food coloring until uniformly colored.

Step 3

Stir flour mixture into butter mixture gradually with electric mixer on low speed until combined; stir in 1 cup chocolate chips. Cover bowl with plastic wrap; place in the refrigerator for 1 hour or up to overnight.

Step 4

Preheat oven to 350 degrees F (175 degrees C). Line baking sheets with parchment paper.

Step 5

Roll dough into 2-inch balls; place on prepared baking sheets and flatten slightly.

Step 6

Bake in the preheated oven until edges are lightly browned, about 10 minutes. Sprinkle cookies with a few additional chocolate chips; allow to cool completely.

Cook's Note:

Chilling the dough is highly recommended; it really does make a difference in the texture of this cookie. You can substitute white chocolate for the dark chocolate chips, for a nice contrast in color. If chilled overnight, remove dough from refrigerator about 30 minutes before working with it.

Nutrition Facts

Per Serving:

205 calories; protein 2.8g 6% DV; carbohydrates 28.9g 9% DV; fat 9.9g 15% DV; cholesterol 28.8mg 10% DV; sodium 232.3mg 9% DV.

Cardamom Rose Meringues

Prep: 15 mins **Cook:** 1 hr 30 mins **Total:** 1 hr 45 mins

Servings: 12

Yield: 12 meringue cookies

Ingredients

- 2 large egg whites egg whites
- ¼ teaspoon cream of tartar
- ⅔ cup white sugar
- ¼ cup water
- 2 teaspoons rose extract
- ¼ teaspoon ground cardamom
- ⅛ teaspoon salt
- 1 drop red food coloring

Directions

Step 1

Preheat oven to 250 degrees F (120 degrees C). Line a baking sheet with parchment paper.

Step 2

In a mixing bowl, beat egg whites and cream of tartar together with an electric mixer on high speed until the mixture forms stiff peaks.

Step 3

Place sugar, water, rose extract, cardamom, salt, and food coloring in a saucepan, and bring to a simmer over low heat, stirring until the sugar has dissolved. Simmer the mixture for a minute or two, stirring constantly, and very slowly pour the syrup in a thin stream into the egg whites, beating constantly with electric mixer on high speed. Beat until the syrup is incorporated and the meringue is stiff and shiny.

Step 4

Drop by spoonfuls or pipe into rosettes with a star tip onto the prepared baking sheet.

Step 5

Bake in the preheated oven until the meringues are hard, 1 to 1 1/2 hours; turn off the oven, and allow them to cool inside the oven to finish baking the insides.

Cook's Notes

Don't make meringues on days with high humidity, or they won't dry right and might collapse.

If using a very liquidy food coloring, reduce the water a little bit -- too much water in the meringues will cause them to leak while baking and form sugary pools at the base.

To substitute rosewater for extract, 1 tablespoon. of rosewater is equal to 1 teaspoon extract. Reduce the water in the recipe if using rosewater.

Nutrition Facts

Per Serving:

46 calories; protein 0.6g 1% DV; carbohydrates 11.2g 4% DV; fatg; cholesterolmg; sodium 33.7mg 1% DV.

No-Bake Chocolate Peanut Butter Bars

Prep: 15 mins **Additional:** 1 hr **Total:** 1 hr 15 mins

Servings: 60

Yield: 60 servings

Ingredients

- 2 cups peanut butter, divided
- ¾ cup butter, softened
- 2 cups powdered sugar
- 3 cups graham cracker crumbs
- 1 (12 ounce) package NESTLE TOLL HOUSE Semi-Sweet Chocolate Mini Morsels, divided

Directions

Step 1

Grease 13 x 9-inch baking pan.

Step 2

Beat 1 1/4 cups peanut butter and butter in large mixer bowl until creamy. Gradually beat in 1 cup powdered sugar. With hands or wooden spoon, work in remaining powdered sugar, graham cracker crumbs and 1/2 cup morsels. Press evenly into prepared baking pan. Smooth top with spatula.

Step 3

Melt remaining peanut butter and remaining morsels in medium, heavy-duty saucepan over lowest possible heat, stirring constantly, until smooth. Spread over graham cracker crust in pan. Refrigerate for at least 1 hour or until chocolate is firm; cut into bars. Store in refrigerator.

Nutrition Facts

Per Serving:

135 calories; protein 2.8g 6% DV; carbohydrates 12.4g 4% DV; fat 8.9g 14% DV; cholesterol 8mg 3% DV; sodium 90.6mg 4% DV.

Easy Red Velvet Sandwich Cookies

Prep: 25 mins **Cook:** 8 mins **Total:** 33 mins

Servings: 24

Yield: 24 cookies

Ingredients

- 1 (18.25 ounce) box red velvet cake mix
- 2 eaches eggs, lightly beaten
- ½ cup vegetable oil
- 1 tablespoon bourbon
- Icing
- 1 (8 ounce) package cream cheese, softened
- ¼ cup butter, softened
- 2 teaspoons evaporated milk
- 1 teaspoon vanilla
- ½ cup flaked coconut
- 4 cups confectioners' sugar
- ½ cup chopped pecans

Directions

Step 1

Preheat the oven to 375 degrees F (190 degrees C).

Step 2

Mix together cake mix, eggs, oil, and bourbon in a large bowl. Roll the dough into balls the size of walnuts. Place 2 inches apart on ungreased baking sheets.

Step 3

Bake in the preheated oven until the tops start to crack, about 8 minutes. Cool in the pans for 10 minutes before removing to cool completely on a wire rack.

Step 4

In a large bowl combine cream cheese, butter, evaporated milk, vanilla, and coconut. Add the confectioners' sugar 1 cup at a time, mixing well with each addition. If consistency is too stiff, add more milk.

Step 5

Place the chopped pecans in a bowl. Spread a generous amount of icing on the bottom of a cookie, sandwich it with another cookie, pressing firmly so that the icing comes all the way out to the edge. Roll the edges of the sandwich cookies in the chopped pecans. Repeat with the remaining cookies.

Cook's Note

You will likely have extra icing after building your sandwich cookies. It will keep it for up to 2 weeks covered tightly in the refrigerator.

Nutrition Facts

Per Serving:

292 calories; protein 2.5g 5% DV; carbohydrates 39.9g 13% DV; fat 14.3g 22% DV; cholesterol 29.1mg 10% DV; sodium 182.1mg 7% DV.

Orange Almond Biscotti

Servings: 12

Yield: 2 dozen

Ingredients

- 2 ¼ cups all-purpose flour
- 1 ¼ cups white sugar
- 1 pinch salt
- 2 teaspoons baking powder
- ½ cup sliced almonds
- 1 tablespoon orange zest

- 3 large eggs egg, beaten
- 1 tablespoon vegetable oil
- ¼ teaspoon almond extract

Directions

Step 1

Preheat oven to 350 degrees F (175 degrees C). Grease and flour a baking sheet.

Step 2

In a large bowl, stir together flour, sugar, baking powder, salt, almonds, and orange zest. Make a well in the center and add the eggs oil, and almond extract. Stir or mix by hand until the mixture forms a ball.

Step 3

Separate dough into 2 pieces and roll each one into a log about 8 inches long. Place logs on prepared baking sheet and flatten so they are about 3/4 inch thick. Bake in preheated oven for 20 to 25 minutes. Cool slightly, and remove from baking sheets. Slice diagonally into 1/2 inch slices with a serrated knife. Set cookies on side back onto the cookie sheet and bake for 10 to 15 more minutes, turning over after half of the time. Finished cookies should be hard and crunchy.

Nutrition Facts

Per Serving:

219 calories; protein 4.8g 10% DV; carbohydrates 39.9g 13% DV; fat 4.6g 7% DV; cholesterol 46.5mg 16% DV; sodium 99.3mg 4% DV.

Sweet Chocolate Caramel Squares

Prep: 20 mins **Cook:** 40 mins **Total:** 1 hr

Servings: 24

Yield: 24 servings

Ingredients

- 1 cup all-purpose flour
- ½ cup butter, softened
- ½ cup brown sugar
- 2 cups chopped pecans
- 1 cup flaked coconut
- 1 (14 ounce) can sweetened condensed milk
- 1 (11 ounce) package individually wrapped caramels (such as Hershey's), unwrapped

- 2 tablespoons milk
- 1 cup chocolate chips

Directions

Step 1

Preheat oven to 350 degrees F (175 degrees C).

Step 2

Mix flour, butter, and brown sugar together in a bowl; press into a 9x13-inch baking dish.

Step 3

Bake in the preheated oven until crust is lightly browned, 12 to 15 minutes.

Step 4

Sprinkle pecans and coconut over crust. Pour sweetened condensed milk over pecans and coconut.

Step 5

Bake in the preheated oven until set, 25 to 30 minutes.

Step 6

Heat caramels and milk together in a small saucepan over medium-low heat until smooth, 2 to 3 minutes. Pour caramel sauce over baked sweetened condensed milk. Sprinkle chocolate chips over caramel. Cool completely before cutting into bars.

Nutrition Facts

Per Serving:

283 calories; protein 3.7g 8% DV; carbohydrates 34.7g 11% DV; fat 15.9g 24% DV; cholesterol 16.7mg 6% DV; sodium 91.3mg 4% DV.

Classic Butter Cookies

Servings: 48

Yield: 3 to 4 dozen

Ingredients

- 2 ½ cups all-purpose flour
- ½ cup white sugar
- 1 cup butter
- 1 egg

- ½ teaspoon almond extract

Directions

Step 1

Cream the butter until light. Gradually add the sugar and beat until light and fluffy. Beat in the egg and almond extract.

Step 2

Gradually blend in the flour. Cover and chill dough for at least 1 hour.

Step 3

Preheat oven to 350 degrees F (175 degrees C).

Step 4

Roll dough out on a lightly floured surface to 1/8 inch thickness. Cut into desired shapes, using lightly floured cookie cutters. Place cookies on ungreased cookie sheets.

Step 5

Bake at 350 degrees F (175 degrees C) for 8 to 12 minutes or until golden. Remove to wire racks to cool completely. Decorate as desired.

Nutrition Facts

Per Serving:

67 calories; protein 0.8g 2% DV; carbohydrates 7.1g 2% DV; fat 4g 6% DV; cholesterol 14mg 5% DV; sodium 28.8mg 1% DV.

Layers Of Love Chocolate Brownies

Prep: 10 mins **Cook:** 30 mins **Additional:** 15 mins **Total:** 55 mins

Servings: 16

Yield: 16 servings

Ingredients

- ¾ cup all-purpose flour
- ¾ cup NESTLE TOLL HOUSE Baking Cocoa

- ¼ teaspoon salt
- ½ cup butter, cut into pieces
- ½ cup granulated sugar
- ½ cup packed brown sugar
- 3 large eggs large eggs, divided
- 2 teaspoons vanilla extract
- 1 cup chopped pecans
- ¾ cup NESTLE TOLL HOUSE Premier White Morsels
- ½ cup caramel ice cream topping
- ¾ cup NESTLE TOLL HOUSE Semi-Sweet Chocolate Morsels

Directions

Step 1

Preheat oven to 350 degrees F. Grease 8-inch-square baking pan.

Step 2

Combine flour, cocoa and salt in small bowl. Beat butter, granulated sugar and brown sugar in large mixer bowl until creamy. Add 2 eggs, one at a time, beating well after each addition. Add vanilla extract; mix well. Gradually beat in flour mixture. Reserve 3/4 cup batter. Spread remaining batter into prepared baking pan. Sprinkle nuts and white morsels over batter. Drizzle caramel topping over top. Beat remaining egg and reserved batter in same large bowl until light in color. Stir in semi-sweet morsels. Spread evenly over caramel topping.

Step 3

Bake for 30 to 35 minutes or until center is set. Cool completely in pan on wire rack. Cut into squares.

Nutrition Facts

Per Serving:

304 calories; protein 4.5g 9% DV; carbohydrates 37.6g 12% DV; fat 16.7g 26% DV; cholesterol 50.2mg 17% DV; sodium 139.8mg 6% DV.

Italian Pizzelles

Servings: 18

Yield: 3 dozen

Ingredients

- ½ cup ground walnuts
- 2 ¼ cups all-purpose flour
- ¼ cup unsweetened cocoa powder
- 1 tablespoon baking powder

- 3 large eggs eggs
- 1 cup white sugar
- ⅓ cup butter, melted
- 2 teaspoons vanilla extract

Directions

Step 1

In a medium bowl, stir together the ground nuts, flour, cocoa and baking powder; set aside. In a separate bowl, beat eggs on the high speed of an electric mixer, gradually add the sugar and mix until thick and yellow. Stir in the melted butter and vanilla. Gradually stir in the flour mixture, just mixing enough to combine.

Step 2

Heat up the pizzelle iron until a drop of water dances on the surface, then slightly reduce heat. Drop 1 rounded tablespoon of batter for each cookie. Close the lid and bake for about 2 minutes, depending on your iron. Turn cookie out and trim before cooling on racks.

Nutrition Facts

Per Serving:

161 calories; protein 3.3g 7% DV; carbohydrates 24.3g 8% DV; fat 6g 9% DV; cholesterol 40mg 13% DV; sodium 117.8mg 5% DV.

Polvorones Rosas (Pink Mexican Sugar Cookies)

Prep: 20 mins **Cook:** 15 mins **Total:** 35 mins

Servings: 24

Yield: 2 dozen large cookies

Ingredients

- 1 cup salted butter, at room temperature
- 1 cup shortening
- 3 teaspoons Mexican vanilla extract
- 1 teaspoon salt
- 2 cups powdered sugar
- 3 drops red food coloring, or as needed
- 4 cups all-purpose flour
- ½ cup red decorator sugar, or as needed

Directions

Step 1

Preheat the oven to 350 degrees F (175 degrees C).

Step 2

Beat butter and shortening with an electric mixer until smooth and creamy. Add vanilla extract and salt. Mix in powdered sugar. Add enough red food coloring to reach the desired shade of pink. Stir in flour until dough is just combined.

Step 3

Scoop 2-inch balls of dough onto a cookie sheet. Dip the bottom of a glass in sugar use it to press dough to 1/2-inch thickness.

Step 4

Bake in the preheated oven until bottoms of cookies are slightly golden brown, 15 to 18 minutes. Dip cookies in decorator sugar while still warm. Transfer to wire racks to cool completely.

Nutrition Facts

Per Serving:

278 calories; protein 2.2g 5% DV; carbohydrates 30.5g 10% DV; fat 16.4g 25% DV; cholesterol 20.3mg 7% DV; sodium 152mg 6% DV.

Love Letters

Prep: 25 mins **Cook:** 8 mins **Total:** 33 mins

Servings: 24

Yield: 4 dozen

Ingredients

- 2 cups all-purpose flour
- ½ cup white sugar
- 1 teaspoon salt
- 1 cup butter
- 2 teaspoons lemon zest
- 1 tablespoon orange zest
- ½ cup sour cream
- 1 cup candied cherries, chopped

Directions

Step 1

Preheat oven to 475 degrees F (245 degrees C).

Step 2

Blend flour, sugar and salt. Cut in butter, lemon zest and orange zest until mixture resembles coarse meal. Blend sour cream in evenly.

Step 3

Gather dough into firm ball. Divide in half. Roll on well-floured surface to 1/8 inch thickness. Cut in 3 x 2 inch pieces; fold ends to center to resemble an envelope, overlapping slightly; seal with tiny piece of candied cherry.

Step 4

Place on ungreased baking sheet. Brush tops with water; sprinkle with sugar. Bake 6 to 8 minutes.

Nutrition Facts

Per Serving:

150 calories; protein 1.3g 3% DV; carbohydrates 16.8g 5% DV; fat 8.8g 14% DV; cholesterol 22.4mg 8% DV; sodium 158.5mg 6% DV.

Chocolate Peppermint Meringue Drops

Prep: 15 mins **Cook:** 30 mins **Additional:** 20 mins **Total:** 1 hr 5 mins

Servings: 30

Yield: 2.5 dozen cookies

Ingredients

- 3 large egg whites egg whites
- ⅛ teaspoon cream of tartar
- 4 drops peppermint oil, or to taste
- ¾ cup white sugar
- 1 drop red food coloring, or as needed
- 3 eaches peppermint candy canes, crushed
- ½ cup chocolate chips

Directions

Step 1

Preheat oven to 300 degrees F (150 degrees C). Line a baking sheet with parchment paper.

Step 2

Beat egg whites, cream of tartar, and peppermint oil together in a mixing bowl with an electric mixer on medium-high speed until soft peaks form. Beat in sugar, about 1 tablespoon at a time; beat in food coloring if desired, until the mixture is glossy and forms stiff peaks. Very gently fold in the crushed candy canes and chocolate chips. Drop the meringue by tablespoon onto the prepared baking sheet.

Step 3

Bake in the preheated oven until dry, 28 to 33 minutes. Cool the cookies on baking sheet on a rack for 20 minutes before removing from parchment paper.

Cook's Note

Add clear vanilla extract if desired and garnish with chocolate chips, red sugar, peppermint pieces, powdered sugar, or cocoa, or do a little of each to create a variety without having to bake several different kinds of cookies!

Nutrition Facts

Per Serving:

45 calories; protein 0.5g 1% DV; carbohydrates 9.5g 3% DV; fat 0.8g 1% DV; cholesterolmg; sodium 6.9mg.

Maraschino Cherry Almond Cookies

Prep: 1 hr **Cook:** 12 mins **Additional:** 18 mins **Total:** 1 hr 30 mins

Servings: 48

Yield: 4 dozen cookies

Ingredients

- 1 cup unsalted butter, at room temperature
- ⅔ cup sifted confectioners' sugar
- 1 ½ teaspoons almond extract
- 2 large eggs eggs, at room temperature
- ⅛ teaspoon salt
- 2 cups all-purpose flour
- ⅔ cup chopped drained maraschino cherries

Royal Icing:

- 2 large egg whites egg whites
- 2 teaspoons lemon juice
- ½ teaspoon vanilla extract
- 3 cups sifted confectioners' sugar

Directions

Step 1

Place the butter in a mixing bowl, and beat with an electric mixer on high speed until smooth and creamy, about 2 minutes. Gradually beat in 2/3 cup of confectioners' sugar, then add almond extract, eggs, and salt, and beat until the mixture is fluffy and well combined, about 3 more minutes. Reduce mixer speed to medium, and gradually beat in flour until the dough is smooth, about 1 minute. Gently stir in the maraschino cherries.

Step 2

Form the dough into 2 logs about 1 inch in diameter, roll each log in plastic wrap or waxed paper, and refrigerate until thoroughly chilled, at least 2 hours.

Step 3

Preheat oven to 350 degrees F (175 degrees C). Line several baking sheets with parchment paper.

Step 4

Cut each dough log into about 25 slices about 1/2-inch thick, and place the cookies on the prepared baking sheets, leaving about 1/2 inch of space between each cookie.

Step 5

Bake in the preheated oven until the cookies are set but not browned, 12 to 14 minutes. Remove to cooling racks to cool to room temperature, about 15 minutes.

Step 6

To make icing, beat egg whites with lemon juice until frothy, about 1 minute, then beat in vanilla extract and confectioners' sugar, a cupful at a time, until the icing is smooth and spreadable. Spread about 1 teaspoon of icing on each cooled cookie, and let the icing harden before stacking.

Cook's Notes

Dough can be made ahead of time and stored in the fridge for 3 days or in the freezer for up to a month until ready to use.

Substitute almond extract for vanilla extract in the icing, if desired, and place slivered almonds on iced cookies before the frosting hardens.

Nutrition Facts

Per Serving:

98 calories; protein 1g 2% DV; carbohydrates 14.6g 5% DV; fat 4g 6% DV; cholesterol 17.9mg 6% DV; sodium 11.5mg 1% DV.

Valentine's Day Strawberry Chocolate Chip Cookies

Prep: 20 mins **Cook:** 10 mins **Additional:** 5 mins **Total:** 35 mins

Servings: 16

Yield: 16 cookies

Ingredients

- 1 (18.25 ounce) package strawberry cake mix
- 1 teaspoon baking powder
- 2 large eggs
- ⅓ cup canola oil
- ½ teaspoon vanilla extract
- 1 ¼ cups semisweet chocolate chips, or more to taste

Directions

Step 1

Preheat the oven to 350 degrees F (175 degrees C). Line a large baking sheet with parchment paper.

Step 2

Mix together cake mix and baking powder in a large bowl and set aside.

Step 3

Whisk together eggs, oil, and vanilla extract in a smaller bowl. Add egg mixture to cake mixture and stir vigorously to form a dough; be sure to incorporate all pockets of dry cake mix. Gently mix in chocolate chips.

Step 4

Drop rounded balls of dough, about 2 1/2 tablespoons each, onto the prepared baking sheet; make balls taller than they are wide. Add 1 or 2 additional chocolate chips onto each cookie, if desired.

Step 5

Bake in the preheated oven for 10 minutes; do not let cookies brown.

Step 6

Allow the soft cookies to cool on the baking sheet for 3 minutes. Cookies will sink as they cool; you can press down gently with your fingers if necessary. Transfer cookies to a wire rack to cool completely. Store in an airtight container for up to 1 week.

Cook's Note:

Be sure to keep an eye on them so they don't brown, this will make them look less pink. Add a few extra chocolate chips on the top to make them look nice.

Nutrition Facts

Per Serving:

188 calories; protein 1.7g 3% DV; carbohydrates 27.4g 9% DV; fat 8.2g 13% DV; cholesterol 23.3mg 8% DV; sodium 239.8mg 10% DV.

Valentine Brownies with Raspberry Coulis

Servings: 5 **Yield:** 4 to 6 servings

Ingredients

- ¼ cup butter
- 2 (1 ounce) squares unsweetened chocolate
- 1 cup white sugar
- 2 large eggs eggs
- ½ teaspoon vanilla extract
- ¼ cup all-purpose flour
- ½ teaspoon salt
- 1 cup chopped walnuts
- 1 (10 ounce) package frozen raspberries
- 1 tablespoon raspberry juice
- 1 ½ teaspoons cornstarch
- 1 tablespoon orange zest

Directions

Step 1

Preheat oven to 325 degrees F (165 degrees C).

Step 2

To make brownies: In a medium saucepan over medium heat, melt butter or margarine and chocolate; take off of heat. Stir in sugar, eggs and vanilla; beat well. Mix in flour, salt and nuts, if desired.

Step 3

In a greased 8x8 inch baking dish, pour brownie mix.

Step 4

Bake in preheated oven for 40 minutes or until toothpick in the center of brownies comes out somewhat clean.

Step 5

To make Raspberry Coulis: In a medium saucepan over medium-high heat, cook raspberries for 5 to 8 minutes; turn down to medium.

Step 6

In a small bowl, combine juice and cornstarch to make a paste; add to raspberries stirring constantly until thickened. Add rind and cool.

Step 7

Pool coulis on a dessert plate and place brownie portion on top of coulis; serve.

Nutrition Facts

Per Serving:

562 calories; protein 8.7g 17% DV; carbohydrates 67.6g 22% DV; fat 32.5g 50% DV; cholesterol 98.8mg 33% DV; sodium 330mg 13% DV.

Muddy Hearts

Prep: 20 mins **Cook:** 7 mins **Total:** 27 mins

Servings: 12

Yield: 12 cookies

Ingredients

- 1 egg
- 1 cup crunchy peanut butter
- 1 cup white sugar
- 1 (12 ounce) package milk chocolate chips

Directions

Step 1

Preheat the oven to 350 degrees F (175 degrees C).

Step 2

Line a baking sheet with parchment paper.

Step 3

Combine egg, peanut butter and sugar in a bowl. The dough should be slightly dry; add small amounts of sugar if it seems too wet.

Step 4

Place dough between two sheets of wax paper and roll to 1/2 inch thickness.

Step 5

Cut the dough with a heart-shaped cookie cutter.

Step 6

Place the hearts on the prepared baking sheet.

Step 7

Bake in the preheated oven until the edges are golden, 7 to 10 minutes.

Step 8

Cool completely on the baking sheet.

Step 9

Melt the chocolate chips in the microwave at 30 second intervals until fully melted, stirring between intervals.

Step 10

Dip the bottom and sides of each cookie in the melted chocolate.

Step 11

Place cookies on wax paper to dry.

Nutrition Facts

Per Serving:

348 calories; protein 7.6g 15% DV; carbohydrates 38.3g 12% DV; fat 20.6g 32% DV; cholesterol 24.9mg 8% DV; sodium 157.5mg 6% DV.

Valentine's Day Cup Cake

REALLY Real Strawberry Cupcakes

Prep: 30 mins **Cook:** 17 mins **Total:** 47 mins

Servings: 20

Yield: 20 standard cupcakes

Ingredients

- 1 ¼ ounces freeze-dried strawberries
- ¾ cup all-purpose flour
- ¾ cup cake flour
- 1 ½ teaspoons baking powder
- ¼ teaspoon baking soda
- ½ teaspoon salt
- ½ cup unsalted butter, room temperature
- 1 ⅓ cups white sugar
- 3 large eggs eggs, room temperature
- 1 teaspoon vanilla extract
- ⅔ cup whole milk, room temperature

Directions

Step 1

Preheat oven to 350 degrees F (175 degrees C). Line muffin tins with 20 cupcake liners (for mini cupcakes, line 72 mini muffin tins).

Step 2

Grind strawberries into a fine powder using a coffee grinder or food processor. Whisk strawberry powder, all-purpose flour, cake flour, baking powder, baking soda, and salt together in a bowl.

Step 3

Beat butter and sugar in a bowl with an electric mixer until light and fluffy. Mixture should be noticeably lighter in color. Add room-temperature eggs one at a time, allowing each egg to blend into butter mixture before adding the next. Beat in vanilla extract.

Step 4

Stir flour mixture, alternately with the milk, into butter mixture until just incorporated. Fill lined tins with cupcake batter.

Step 5

Bake in preheated oven until cupcakes spring back when gently touched with a fingertip or a toothpick inserted in the center comes out clean, 16 to 18 minutes for regular cupcakes, 8 to 10 minutes for mini cupcakes.

Cook's Notes:

To make strawberry powder: grind 1 to 1.6 oz (depending on your taste) freeze-dried strawberries into a fine powder using a coffee grinder, Magic Bullet or food processor. You can find freeze-dried strawberries at Trader Joe's or online, or make your own dried strawberries.

Dry 1 pound of very thinly sliced fresh strawberries in a 180 degrees F (80 degrees C) oven for 8 hours, then grind as above into a fine powder.

Try topping these cupcakes with Real Strawberry Frosting.

Nutrition Facts

Per Serving:

145 calories; protein 2.2g 4% DV; carbohydrates 21.6g 7% DV; fat 5.7g 9% DV; cholesterol 40.9mg 14% DV; sodium 125mg 5% DV.

"Zuccotto" Cupcakes

Prep: 45 mins **Cook:** 15 mins **Additional:** 2 hrs **Total:** 3 hrs

Servings: 24

Yield: 2 dozen cupcakes

Ingredients

For Cupcakes:

- 1 (18.25 ounce) package white cake mix with pudding
- ⅓ cup vegetable oil
- 3 eaches egg whites
- 1 ¼ cups water
- 6 ounces bittersweet chocolate, chopped fine

For Filling:

- 1 cup cold heavy whipping cream
- 2 tablespoons confectioners' sugar
- ½ cup frozen unsweetened raspberries
- ¼ cup chocolate-coated toffee bits
- ½ cup finely chopped toasted hazelnuts, skins removed

For Ganache:

- ½ cup heavy cream
- 6 ounces semisweet chocolate, chopped

For Frosting:

- 1 (12 ounce) package white chocolate chips
- 1 cup unsalted butter, at room temperature
- 2 (8 ounce) packages cream cheese, softened
- 2 teaspoons vanilla extract
- 3 drops food coloring, if desired

Directions

Step 1

Preheat an oven to 350 degrees F (175 degrees C). Line muffin tins with 24 cupcake liners.

Step 2

Combine the cake mix, oil, egg whites, and water in a mixing bowl. Beat with an electric mixer on low speed for 30 seconds, then increase the speed to medium and beat for 2 minutes, scraping down the sides of the bowl. Stir in the chopped bittersweet chocolate and scoop the batter into the cupcake liners, filling them two-thirds full.

Step 3

Bake in the preheated oven until golden and the tops spring back when lightly pressed, 15 to 20 minutes. A toothpick inserted into the center of a cupcake should come out clean. Remove the cupcakes from the pans and cool completely on wire racks.

Step 4

Beat 1 cup cold whipping cream on medium-high speed until the cream has thickened, about 1 minute. Add confectioners' sugar and beat until stiff peaks form. Stir in the frozen raspberries, toffee bits, and chopped toasted hazelnuts.

Step 5

Remove the centers of the cupcakes using an apple corer or paring knife, cutting out the middles in a funnel shape by holding the knife at a 45-degree angle. Spoon or pipe the filling into the cupcakes. Refrigerate the cupcakes while you prepare the ganache.

Step 6

Place the semisweet chocolate pieces in a heat-safe bowl. Bring 1/2 cup heavy cream to a boil. Pour the hot cream over the chocolate; cover the bowl and set aside for 5 minutes. Whisk the chocolate and cream until well combined; allow the ganache to cool until it reaches a spreadable consistency, about 1 hour. Spread a spoonful of ganache evenly over each cupcake. Refrigerate the cupcakes while you prepare the frosting.

Step 7

Melt the white chocolate chips in a microwave-safe bowl by heating for 1 minute, stirring after 30 seconds. Allow the white chocolate to cool until almost room temperature but still fluid. Cream the butter and cream cheese together. Blend in the melted white chocolate, vanilla extract, and food coloring (if using). Spread the frosting on the cupcakes. Serve immediately, or refrigerate until serving.

Cook's Notes

If toasted hazelnuts aren't available at your local grocery or health food store, simply roast raw hazelnuts in a 350 degree F oven (175 degrees C) until the skins crack, 5 to 6 minutes. Remove skins by rubbing vigorously in a clean kitchen towel.

You can use fresh raspberries instead of frozen. If you're using frozen raspberries, don't thaw them first: thawed raspberries will fall apart and weep into the whipped cream mixture. You may also use all bittersweet or semisweet chocolate instead of both types.

Nutrition Facts

Per Serving:

487 calories; protein 5.3g 11% DV; carbohydrates 37.9g 12% DV; fat 36.2g 56% DV; cholesterol 66.3mg 22% DV; sodium 241.7mg 10% DV.

Pineapple Upside Down Cupcakes

Prep: 20 mins **Cook:** 20 mins **Additional:** 5 mins **Total:** 45 mins

Servings: 24

Yield: 2 dozen cupcakes

Ingredients

- cooking spray
- ½ cup butter, melted
- 1 ½ cups brown sugar
- 24 cherries maraschino cherries
- 1 (20 ounce) can crushed pineapple
- 1 (18.25 ounce) package pineapple cake mix (such as Duncan Hines Pineapple Supreme)
- 3 large eggs eggs
- 1 ⅓ cups pineapple juice
- ⅓ cup vegetable oil
- 1 tablespoon confectioners' sugar for dusting, or as needed

Directions

Step 1

Move an oven rack into the middle of the oven. Preheat oven to 350 degrees F (175 degrees C).

Step 2

Spray 24 muffin cups with cooking spray.

Step 3

Line a work surface with waxed paper.

Step 4

Spoon 1 teaspoon melted butter into the bottom of each sprayed muffin cup.

Step 5

Spoon 1 tablespoon brown sugar in each muffin cup.

Step 6

Press a maraschino cherry into the center of the brown sugar in each muffin cup.

Step 7

Spoon a heaping tablespoon of crushed pineapple over the cherry and compact it with the back of a spoon into an even layer.

Step 8

Mix pineapple cake mix, eggs, pineapple juice, and vegetable oil in a large bowl with electric mixer on low speed until moistened, about 30 seconds. Turn mixer speed to medium and mix for 2 minutes.

Step 9

Pour pineapple cake batter into the muffin cups, filling them to the top; do not overfill.

Step 10

Bake in the preheated oven until a toothpick inserted into the center of a cupcake comes out clean, about 20 minutes.

Step 11

Allow cupcakes to cool at least 5 minutes before inverting muffin cups onto the waxed paper to release. Serve with pineapple and cherry sides up. Sprinkle cupcakes lightly with confectioners' sugar.

Nutrition Facts

Per Serving:

237 calories; protein 1.5g 3% DV; carbohydrates 38.6g 12% DV; fat 9g 14% DV; cholesterol 33.4mg 11% DV; sodium 174.1mg 7% DV.

Cupcake Princess' Vanilla Cupcakes

Prep: 15 mins **Cook:** 20 mins **Additional:** 1 hr 10 mins **Total:** 1 hr 45 mins

Servings: 12

Ingredients

- 1 ¼ cups all-purpose flour
- ¾ teaspoon baking soda
- 1 pinch salt
- 5 tablespoons butter, cut into pieces
- ⅔ cup milk
- 1 cup white sugar
- 2 large eggs eggs
- 1 egg yolk
- 1 teaspoon vanilla extract

Directions

Step 1

Preheat an oven to 350 degrees F (175 degrees C). Line a standard muffin tin with 12 paper cupcake liners. Combine flour, baking soda, and salt in a bowl; set aside.

Step 2

Heat the butter and milk in a small saucepan over low heat until the butter has melted. Beat the sugar, eggs, egg yolk, and vanilla with an electric mixer in a large bowl until it has thickened slightly and is lighter in color. Gradually beat in the flour mixture on low speed until just incorporated. Slowly pour in the hot milk, beating until just combined.

Step 3

Divide batter evenly between cupcake liners. Bake until toothpick inserted into center comes out clean, about 20 minutes. Cool cupcakes in pan for 10 minutes. Transfer cupcakes to a cooling rack to cool completely.

Cook's Note

If you want to double this recipe just use 5 whole eggs instead of 4 eggs plus 2 egg yolks to make your life easier.

Nutrition Facts

Per Serving:

178 calories; protein 3.1g 6% DV; carbohydrates 27.4g 9% DV; fat 6.4g 10% DV; cholesterol 61.9mg 21% DV; sodium 130.9mg 5% DV.

Red Velvet Cupcakes

Prep: 20 mins **Cook:** 20 mins **Additional:** 20 mins **Total:** 1 hr

Servings: 12

Yield: 1 dozen cupcakes

Ingredients

Dry ingredients:

- 1 ⅓ cups all-purpose flour
- 3 tablespoons unsweetened cocoa powder
- ¼ teaspoon baking soda
- ½ teaspoon salt
- 1 teaspoon baking powder

Wet ingredients:

- ¼ cup butter, softened
- 1 cup white sugar
- 2 large eggs large eggs
- ¾ cup buttermilk
- 2 teaspoons white vinegar
- 1 teaspoon vanilla extract
- 1 tablespoon red food coloring

Directions

Step 1

Preheat oven to 350 degrees F (175 degrees C). Line 12 muffin cups with paper liners.

Step 2

Sift flour, cocoa, baking soda, salt, and baking powder together in a large mixing bowl until combined.

Step 3

Place butter and sugar into the work bowl of a large stand mixer fitted with a whisk attachment. Beat butter and sugar together until light and fluffy. Scrape down attachment and bowl. Add eggs into butter-sugar mixture, one at a time, mixing the first egg in thoroughly before adding the second. Scrape down sides of bowl as you work.

Step 4

Beat buttermilk and vinegar into moist ingredients, followed by vanilla extract and red food coloring. Mix until color is even.

Step 5

Pour dry ingredients into wet ingredients and gently whisk by hand until batter is smooth. Spoon batter into prepared muffin cups, filling them about 3/4 full.

Step 6

Bake in the preheated oven until a toothpick inserted into the center of a cupcake comes out clean, 20 to 25 minutes. Let sit in the pan for 10 minutes; remove cupcakes from pan and cool completely on a cooling rack before frosting. Unwrap cupcakes before frosting.

Cook's Note:

I like to dust frosted cupcakes with a little bit of cocoa powder, just to make them look even cooler.

Nutrition Facts

Per Serving:

171 calories; protein 3.3g 7% DV; carbohydrates 29g 9% DV; fat 5.1g 8% DV; cholesterol 41.8mg 14% DV; sodium 219.3mg 9% DV.

CINfully Delicious Chocolate Cupcakes

Prep: 20 mins **Cook:** 15 mins **Additional:** 30 mins **Total:** 1 hr 5 mins

Servings: 24

Yield: 2 dozen cupcakes

Ingredients

- 1 (18.25 ounce) package chocolate cake mix
- 1 cup milk
- 3 large eggs eggs
- ½ cup butter, melted
- 1 teaspoon ground cinnamon

- 1 teaspoon vanilla extract
- 1 teaspoon cinnamon sugar, or as needed
- ½ cup butter
- ½ cup butter-flavored shortening
- 1 pinch sea salt
- 1 teaspoon vanilla extract
- 1 tablespoon ground cinnamon
- 1 tablespoon unsweetened cocoa powder
- 3 cups confectioners' sugar
- ¼ cup milk
- 2 cups confectioners' sugar, or more as needed

Directions

Step 1

Preheat an oven to 350 degrees F (175 degrees C).

Step 2

Line 24 muffin cups with paper liners.

Step 3

Beat together the chocolate cake mix, 1 cup milk, eggs, 1/2 cup melted butter, 1 teaspoon cinnamon, and 1 teaspoon vanilla extract in a bowl with an electric mixer on low speed until moist. Beat for 2 more minutes on medium speed.

Step 4

Fill each muffin cup about 2/3 full of batter.

Step 5

Sprinkle the cupcakes with cinnamon sugar.

Step 6

Bake in the preheated oven until a toothpick inserted into the center comes out clean, about 15 minutes.

Step 7

Cool in the pans for 10 minutes before removing to cool completely on a wire rack.

Step 8

Cream together 1/2 cup butter and shortening in a bowl until smooth.

Step 9

Stir in sea salt, 1 teaspoon vanilla extract, 1 tablespoon cinnamon, cocoa powder, and 3 cups confectioners' sugar.

Step 10

Stir in milk.

Step 11

Mix in 2 more cups confectioners' sugar or as needed until desired consistency is achieved.

Step 12

Spread the frosting on the cooled cupcakes.

Nutrition Facts

Per Serving:

320 calories; protein 2.6g 5% DV; carbohydrates 43g 14% DV; fat 16.4g 25% DV; cholesterol 44.6mg 15% DV; sodium 259.9mg 10% DV.

Mascarpone Strawberry Cupcakes

Prep: 15 mins **Cook:** 20 mins **Total:** 35 mins

Servings: 12

Yield: 1 dozen cupcakes

Ingredients

- 1 (18.25 ounce) package moist white cake mix
- 1 cup water
- 1 (8 ounce) container mascarpone cheese
- ¼ cup vegetable oil
- 2 large egg whites egg whites
- ½ cup frozen strawberries, thawed
- 2 ½ cups confectioners' sugar

Directions

Step 1

Preheat oven to 350 degrees F (175 degrees C).

Step 2

Line 12 muffin cups with liners.

Step 3

Stir cake mix, water, mascarpone cheese, vegetable oil, and egg whites in a bowl until well combined.

Step 4

Pour cake mixture into prepared muffin cups.

Step 5

Bake in preheated oven until lightly browned, about 20 minutes.

Step 6

Place strawberries in a food processor or blender; puree until smooth.

Step 7

Stir pureed strawberries and confectioners' sugar together in a bowl.

Step 8

Spoon strawberry mixture on top of cupcakes.

Nutrition Facts

Per Serving:

409 calories; protein 3.9g 8% DV; carbohydrates 60.1g 19% DV; fat 17.9g 28% DV; cholesterol 23.3mg 8% DV; sodium 303mg 12% DV.

Light and Airy Strawberry Cupcakes

Prep: 10 mins **Cook:** 20 mins **Total:** 30 mins

Servings: 12

Yield: 1 dozen cupcakes

Ingredients

- 2 cups all-purpose flour
- 1 cup white sugar
- 2 teaspoons baking soda
- 1 cup water
- 1 cup mayonnaise
- 2 ½ tablespoons strawberry preserves
- 1 teaspoon vanilla extract
- 12 large fresh strawberries

Directions

Step 1

Preheat oven to 350 degrees F (175 degrees C). Grease 12 muffin cups or line with paper liners.

Step 2

Stir flour, sugar, and baking soda together in a large bowl; make a well in the center. Add water, mayonnaise, strawberry preserves, and vanilla extract to the well and mix until batter is just blended. Spoon batter into the prepared muffin cups. Press 1 strawberry into each.

Step 3

Bake in the preheated oven until tops spring back when pressed, 20 to 25 minutes.

Cook's Note:

Sift dry ingredients before adding wet ingredients to make cupcakes lighter and airier.

Nutrition Facts

Per Serving:

289 calories; protein 2.4g 5% DV; carbohydrates 37.3g 12% DV; fat 14.8g 23% DV; cholesterol 7mg 2% DV; sodium 315.1mg 13% DV.

Black Bottom Cupcakes

Prep: 30 mins **Cook:** 30 mins **Total:** 1 hr

Servings: 24

Yield: 2 dozen cupcakes

Ingredients

- 1 (8 ounce) package cream cheese, softened
- 1 egg
- ⅓ cup white sugar
- ⅛ teaspoon salt
- 1 cup miniature semisweet chocolate chips
- 1 ½ cups all-purpose flour
- 1 cup white sugar
- ¼ cup unsweetened cocoa powder
- 1 teaspoon baking soda
- ½ teaspoon salt
- 1 cup water
- ⅓ cup vegetable oil
- 1 tablespoon cider vinegar
- 1 teaspoon vanilla extract

Directions

Step 1

Preheat oven to 350 degrees F (175 degrees C). Line muffin tins with paper cups or lightly spray with non-stick cooking spray.

Step 2

In a medium bowl, beat the cream cheese, egg, 1/3 cup sugar and 1/8 teaspoon salt until light and fluffy. Stir in the chocolate chips and set aside.

Step 3

In a large bowl, mix together the flour, 1 cup sugar, cocoa, baking soda and 1/2 teaspoon salt. Make a well in the center and add the water, oil, vinegar and vanilla. Stir together until well blended. Fill muffin tins 1/3 full with the batter and top with a dollop of the cream cheese mixture.

Step 4

Bake in preheated oven for 25 to 30 minutes.

Nutrition Facts

Per Serving:

171 calories; protein 2.3g 5% DV; carbohydrates 22.4g 7% DV; fat 8.9g 14% DV; cholesterol 18mg 6% DV; sodium 145mg 6% DV.

Cream Filled Cupcakes

Prep: 15 mins **Cook:** 20 mins **Additional:** 15 mins **Total:** 50 mins

Servings: 36

Yield: 36 cupcakes

Ingredients

- 3 cups all-purpose flour
- 2 cups white sugar
- ⅓ cup unsweetened cocoa powder
- 2 teaspoons baking soda
- 1 teaspoon salt
- 2 large eggs eggs
- 1 cup milk
- 1 cup water
- 1 cup vegetable oil
- 1 teaspoon vanilla extract
- ¼ cup butter
- ¼ cup shortening

- 2 cups confectioners' sugar
- 1 pinch salt

- 3 tablespoons milk
- 1 teaspoon vanilla extract

Directions

Step 1

Preheat oven to 375 degrees F (190 degrees C). Line 36 muffin cups with paper liners.

Step 2

In a large bowl, mix together the flour, sugar, cocoa, baking soda and 1 teaspoon salt. Make a well in the center and pour in the eggs, 1 cup milk, water, oil and 1 teaspoon vanilla. Mix well. Fill each muffin cup half-full of batter.

Step 3

Bake in the preheated oven for 15 to 20 minutes, or until a toothpick inserted into the center of the cake comes out clean. Allow to cool.

Step 4

Make filling: In a large bowl, beat butter and shortening together until smooth. Blend in confectioners' sugar and pinch of salt. Gradually beat in 3 tablespoons milk and 1 teaspoon vanilla. beat until light and fluffy. Fill a pastry bag with a small tip. Push tip through bottom of paper liner to fill each cupcake.

Nutrition Facts

Per Serving:

196 calories; protein 1.9g 4% DV; carbohydrates 26.9g 9% DV; fat 9.4g 15% DV; cholesterol 14.4mg 5% DV; sodium 151.4mg 6% DV.

Moist Red Velvet Cupcakes

Prep: 30 mins **Cook:** 20 mins **Total:** 50 mins

Servings: 20

Yield: 20 cupcakes

Ingredients

- ½ cup butter
- 1 ½ cups white sugar

- 2 large eggs eggs
- 1 cup buttermilk

- 1 fluid ounce red food coloring
- 1 teaspoon vanilla extract
- 1 ½ teaspoons baking soda
- 1 tablespoon distilled white vinegar
- 2 cups all-purpose flour
- ⅓ cup unsweetened cocoa powder
- 1 teaspoon salt

Directions

Step 1

Preheat oven to 350 degrees F (175 degrees C). Grease two 12 cup muffin pans or line with 20 paper baking cups.

Step 2

In a large bowl, beat the butter and sugar with an electric mixer until light and fluffy. Mix in the eggs, buttermilk, red food coloring and vanilla. Stir in the baking soda and vinegar. Combine the flour, cocoa powder and salt; stir into the batter just until blended. Spoon the batter into the prepared cups, dividing evenly.

Step 3

Bake in the preheated oven until the tops spring back when lightly pressed, 20 to 25 minutes. Cool in the pan set over a wire rack. When cool, arrange the cupcakes on a serving platter and frost with desired frosting.

Nutrition Facts

Per Serving:

160 calories; protein 2.7g 5% DV; carbohydrates 26g 8% DV; fat 5.5g 9% DV; cholesterol 31.3mg 10% DV; sodium 263.8mg 11% DV.

Black Bottom Cupcakes

Servings: 24

Yield: 18 to 24 servings

Ingredients

- 1 (8 ounce) package cream cheese
- 1 egg
- ⅓ cup white sugar
- ⅛ teaspoon salt
- 1 cup semisweet chocolate chips
- 1 ½ cups all-purpose flour
- 1 cup white sugar
- ¼ cup cocoa
- 1 teaspoon baking soda
- ½ teaspoon salt

- 1 cup water
- ⅓ cup vegetable oil

- 1 tablespoon distilled white vinegar
- 1 teaspoon vanilla extract

Directions

Step 1

Preheat oven to 350 degrees F (175 degrees C). Lightly butter muffin tins and set aside.

Step 2

Beat together the cream cheese, egg, sugar and salt. Stir in chocolate chips and set aside.

Step 3

In a separate bowl, sift together the flour, sugar, cocoa, baking soda and salt. Add the water, oil, vinegar, and vanilla. Beat until well combined. Batter will be thin.

Step 4

Fill muffin cups 1/3 full with the chocolate batter. Top each one with a spoonful of cream cheese mixture.

Step 5

Bake for 30 to 35 minutes.

Nutrition Facts

Per Serving:

172 calories; protein 2.5g 5% DV; carbohydrates 22.4g 7% DV; fat 8.7g 13% DV; cholesterol 18mg 6% DV; sodium 144.2mg 6% DV.

Almond Cupcake with Salted Caramel Buttercream Frosting

Prep: 30 mins **Cook:** 25 mins **Additional:** 30 mins **Total:** 1 hr 25 mins

Servings: 12

Yield: 1 dozen cupcakes

Ingredients

- 1 ½ cups all-purpose flour

- 1 ¾ teaspoons baking powder

- 1 cup white sugar
- ½ cup margarine, softened
- 2 large eggs eggs
- 1 teaspoon vanilla extract
- 1 teaspoon almond extract
- ¾ cup whole milk
- ½ cup brown sugar

- ½ cup margarine
- 2 tablespoons light corn syrup
- 1 tablespoon vanilla extract
- ½ cup heavy cream, or as needed
- 1 pinch salt
- ¾ cup salted butter, softened
- 2 cups confectioners' sugar, sifted

Directions

Step 1

Preheat oven to 350 degrees F (175 degrees C). Line 12 cupcake cups with paper liners. In a bowl, whisk together the flour and baking powder.

Step 2

In a mixing bowl, thoroughly cream together the sugar and 1/2 cup of margarine until very well blended. Beat in the eggs, one at a time, until thoroughly combined, and stir in the vanilla and almond extracts. Gradually beat in the flour mixture, alternating with the milk, in several additions. Spoon the batter into the prepared cupcake cups, filling them about 2/3 full.

Step 3

Bake the cupcakes in the preheated oven until a toothpick inserted into the center of a cupcake comes out clean, 20 to 25 minutes.

Step 4

To make caramel, Place the brown sugar, 1/2 cup margarine, corn syrup, and vanilla into a large saucepan over medium heat, and bring the mixture to a boil. Reduce heat, and simmer until thickened, 3 to 4 minutes; remove from heat and allow to cool to warm (not hot) temperature. Add the cream, a little at a time, until the caramel has the consistency of honey. Mix in the pinch of salt, and allow to cool to room temperature.

Step 5

Beat the salted butter with confectioners' sugar in a bowl with an electric mixer on medium speed until the mixture is fluffy; slowly add and beat in the caramel, a tablespoon at a time, beating until the frosting is smooth.

Cook's Notes:

Butter can be substituted for margarine, of course, but that's just what I used. The milk could be any type; I used whole milk.

If desired, save back a tablespoon or so of the caramel from the frosting, for a drizzle over the top of the cupcakes.

Nutrition Facts

Per Serving:

526 calories; protein 3.6g 7% DV; carbohydrates 62.5g 20% DV; fat 29.8g 46% DV; cholesterol 69.8mg 23% DV; sodium 353.1mg 14% DV.

Real Strawberry Cupcakes

Prep: 40 mins **Cook:** 25 mins **Additional:** 10 mins **Total:** 1 hr 15 mins

Servings: 12

Yield: 12 cupcakes

Ingredients

- 8 large fresh strawberries, or as needed
- 2 large eggs eggs
- 1 cup white sugar
- ⅓ cup vegetable oil
- ½ teaspoon vanilla extract
- ½ teaspoon lemon zest
- 1 ½ cups all-purpose flour
- 2 teaspoons baking powder
- ¼ teaspoon salt
- 3 tablespoons instant vanilla pudding mix
- 1 drop red food coloring, or as needed
- ¾ cup cream cheese, softened
- 2 tablespoons butter, softened
- ½ cup confectioners' sugar
- ½ teaspoon vanilla extract
- 3 large fresh strawberries, sliced

Directions

Step 1

Preheat oven to 325 degrees F (165 degrees C). Spray cupcake cups with cooking spray, or line with cupcake liners.

Step 2

Place 8 strawberries into a blender, and blend until smooth. Pour the puree through a strainer to remove seeds. Puree should equal about 3/4 cup. Set the puree aside.

Step 3

In a large bowl, beat together the eggs, white sugar, vegetable oil, 1/2 teaspoon vanilla extract, lemon zest, and strawberry puree until well combined. Stir in the flour, baking powder, salt, vanilla pudding mix (for a moister cupcake), and red food coloring to reach a desired shade of pink. Spoon the batter into the prepared cupcake cups, filling each about 2/3 full.

Step 4

Bake in the preheated oven until the cupcakes have risen and a toothpick inserted into the center of a cupcake comes out clean, about 23 minutes. Allow the cupcakes to cool at least 10 minutes before frosting.

Step 5

To make frosting, beat cream cheese and butter together in a mixing bowl with an electric mixer until smooth, and mix in confectioners' sugar and 1/2 teaspoon vanilla extract to make a lump-free icing. Frost each cupcake with about 2 tablespoons of icing, and top each cupcake with a strawberry slice.

Nutrition Facts

Per Serving:

295 calories; protein 3.9g 8% DV; carbohydrates 39g 13% DV; fat 14.1g 22% DV; cholesterol 52mg 17% DV; sodium 248.9mg 10% DV.

Chocolate Surprise Cupcakes

Prep: 30 mins **Cook:** 25 mins **Total:** 55 mins

Servings: 24

Yield: 24 cupcakes

Ingredients

- 3 cups all-purpose flour
- 2 cups white sugar
- ½ cup unsweetened cocoa powder
- 1 teaspoon salt
- 2 teaspoons baking soda
- ⅔ cup vegetable oil
- 2 cups water
- 2 tablespoons vinegar
- 2 teaspoons vanilla extract
- 1 (8 ounce) package cream cheese, softened
- 1 egg
- ½ cup white sugar
- ¼ teaspoon salt
- 1 cup semisweet chocolate chips

Directions

Step 1

Preheat oven to 350 degrees F (175 degrees C). Line 24 muffin cups with paper liners.

Step 2

In a large bowl, mix together flour, 2 cups sugar, cocoa, 1 teaspoon salt and baking soda. Stir in oil, water, vinegar and vanilla until blended. Pour mixture into prepared muffin cups, filling each 2/3 full.

Step 3

To make the filling: In a medium bowl, beat together the cream cheese, egg, 1/2 cup sugar and 1/4 teaspoon salt until light and fluffy. Stir in chocolate chips. Drop a heaping teaspoonful of the cream cheese mixture into each cupcake. Bake in the preheated oven for 25 minutes. Allow to cool.

Nutrition Facts

Per Serving:

265 calories; protein 3.2g 7% DV; carbohydrates 38.5g 12% DV; fat 12g 19% DV; cholesterol 18mg 6% DV; sodium 258.6mg 10% DV.

Raspberry White Chocolate Buttercream Cupcakes

Prep: 30 mins **Cook:** 25 mins **Additional:** 45 mins **Total:** 1 hr 40 mins

Servings: 24

Yield: 2 dozen cupcakes

Ingredients

- 1 (18.25 ounce) package vanilla cake mix
- 1 cup water
- ⅓ cup vegetable oil
- 3 large eggs eggs
- 8 ounces fresh raspberries
- 1 tablespoon water
- 3 tablespoons white sugar
- 1 tablespoon cornstarch
- ¼ cup water
- 2 cups white chocolate chips
- 1 cup butter
- 5 cups confectioners' sugar
- 2 tablespoons milk, or as needed

Directions

Step 1

Preheat oven to 350 degrees F (175 degrees C).

Step 2

Grease 24 muffin cups or line with paper liners.

Step 3

Mix together vanilla cake mix, 1 cup water, vegetable oil, and eggs in a mixing bowl with an electric mixer on low speed until cake mix is moist. Raise mixer speed to medium and beat until batter is smooth, 2 minutes.

Step 4

Spoon batter into prepared muffin cups, filling them about 2/3 full.

Step 5

Bake in the preheated oven until cupcakes are very lightly browned and a toothpick inserted into the center of a cupcake comes out clean, 18 to 23 minutes.

Step 6

Cool cupcakes in the pans for 5 minutes; transfer cupcakes to cooling rack to finish cooling.

Step 7

Place raspberries, 1 tablespoon water, and white sugar in a blender and pulse several times to chop raspberries; blend until pureed, about 30 seconds.

Step 8

Whisk cornstarch with 1/4 cup water until thoroughly combined; pour mixture into the raspberry mixture in the blender and blend again until smooth.

Step 9

Pour raspberry mixture into a saucepan and simmer over low heat until thickened, about 5 minutes. Let the raspberry filling cool.

Step 10

Cut a core out of each cupcake about 1 1/2 inches long and 1 inch in diameter.

Step 11

Spoon about 2 teaspoons raspberry filling into each cupcake.

Step 12

Place white chocolate chips in a microwave-safe bowl and heat in 30-second intervals until chips begin to melt, about 1 minute. Stir and repeat, heating chips about 10 seconds at a time, until thoroughly melted. Stir until chocolate is smooth and no more lumps remain.

Step 13

Beat butter with an electric mixer on medium speed in a mixing bowl until fluffy. Beat in half the confectioners' sugar, melted white chocolate chips, and milk until mixture is smooth and creamy.

Step 14

Slowly beat in remaining confectioners' sugar until smooth; if frosting is too stiff, beat in more milk, 1 teaspoon at a time.

Step 15

Spread or pipe the white chocolate frosting over the cupcakes to cover the raspberry filling; drizzle or pipe any remaining raspberry filling over cupcakes.

Cook's Note:

If using a piping bag and decorative tip to ice the cupcakes, make sure that the white chocolate is completely melted and there are no small chunks.

Nutrition Facts

Per Serving:

393 calories; protein 3g 6% DV; carbohydrates 54.1g 18% DV; fat 19g 29% DV; cholesterol 46.9mg 16% DV; sodium 221.7mg 9% DV.

Simple 'N' Delicious Chocolate Cake

Prep: 15 mins **Cook:** 35 mins **Additional:** 30 mins **Total:** 1 hr 20 mins

Servings: 8

Yield: 1 8-inch pan

Ingredients

- 1 cup white sugar
- 1.063 cups all-purpose flour

- ½ cup unsweetened cocoa powder
- 1 teaspoon baking soda
- 1 teaspoon salt
- ½ cup butter
- 1 egg
- 1 teaspoon vanilla extract
- 1 cup cold, strong, brewed coffee

Directions

Step 1

Preheat oven to 350 degrees F (175 degrees C). Grease and flour an 8-inch pan (see Editor's Note). Sift together flour, cocoa, baking soda and salt. Set aside.

Step 2

In a medium bowl, cream butter and sugar until light and fluffy. Add egg and vanilla and beat well. Add flour mixture, alternating with coffee. Beat until just incorporated.

Step 3

Bake at 350 degrees F (175 degrees C) for 35 to 45 minutes, or until a toothpick inserted into the cake comes out clean. Allow to cool before frosting.

Nutrition Facts

Per Serving:

282 calories; protein 3.7g 7% DV; carbohydrates 40.7g 13% DV; fat 13g 20% DV; cholesterol 53.8mg 18% DV; sodium 540.6mg 22% DV.

Sweetheart Cupcakes

Prep: 20 mins **Cook:** 20 mins **Additional:** 1 hr

Total: 1 hr 40 mins

Servings: 24

Yield: 2 dozen cupcakes

Ingredients

- 1 (18.25 ounce) package white cake mix
- 1 ¼ cups water
- ⅓ cup vegetable oil
- 3 eaches egg whites
- 8 drops red food coloring
- 2 drops raspberry candy oil

Directions

Step 1

Preheat an oven to 350 degrees F (175 degrees C). Line a standard muffin tin with paper cupcake liners.

Step 2

Beat the cake mix, water, vegetable oil, and egg whites together on low speed for 30 seconds, then on medium for 2 minutes, until smooth. Fill cupcake liners 1/3 full with white batter; set aside.

Step 3

Stir 4 drops of red food coloring into the remaining bowl of batter to make the batter pink. Stir in the raspberry oil. Pour 1/3 of pink batter into a resealable plastic bag and set aside.

Step 4

Mix more food coloring into the remaining bowl of pink batter until it is an orange/red color and pour the batter into a resealable plastic bag. Cut a corner off the bag, stick the open tip into the center of each cup of white batter and squeeze in about two tablespoons of red batter.

Step 5

Cut the corner off the bag with the pink batter, stick the open tip into the center of the red batter and squeeze about 1 tablespoon pink batter into each cup.

Step 6

Bake the layered cupcakes in the preheated oven until a toothpick inserted into the center comes out clean, 15 to 20 minutes. Cool completely before frosting.

Cook's Note:

Top cupcakes with your favorite frosting. I used Sturdy Whipped Cream Frosting from this site.

Nutrition Facts

Per Serving:

120 calories; protein 1.4g 3% DV; carbohydrates 16.6g 5% DV; fat 5.3g 8% DV; cholesterolmg; sodium 148.7mg 6% DV.

Mini Cherry Cheesecakes

Prep: 15 mins **Cook:** 15 mins **Additional:** 1 hr 30 mins **Total:** 2 hrs

Servings: 24

Yield: 2 dozen mini cheesecakes

Ingredients

- 24 wafers vanilla wafer cookies
- 2 (8 ounce) packages cream cheese, softened
- ¾ cup white sugar
- 2 large eggs eggs
- 2 ½ tablespoons lemon juice
- 1 teaspoon vanilla extract
- 1 (12 ounce) can cherry pie filling

Directions

Step 1

Preheat oven to 350 degrees F (175 degrees C). Line 24 muffin cups with paper liners.

Step 2

Place a vanilla wafer into the bottom of each muffin cup.

Step 3

Beat cream cheese, sugar, eggs, lemon juice, and vanilla extract in a bowl until fluffy. Spoon mixture into the muffin cups, filling them 2/3 full.

Step 4

Bake in the preheated oven until cheesecake filling is set, 15 to 20 minutes. Let cool completely, about 1 1/2 hours. Spoon 2 or 3 cherries from pie filling over each cheesecake.

Cook's Note:

I've made this with vegan wafers and dairy-free cream cheese for a friend with a milk allergy. She loved it.

Nutrition Facts

Per Serving:

141 calories; protein 2.2g 5% DV; carbohydrates 15.1g 5% DV; fat 8.1g 13% DV; cholesterol 36mg 12% DV; sodium 82mg 3% DV.

Cherry Cheesecake Cupcakes

Prep: 15 mins **Cook:** 10 mins **Additional:** 30 mins **Total:** 55 mins

Servings: 24

Yield: 24 cupcakes

Ingredients

Crust:

- 1 cup graham cracker crumbs
- ¾ cup butter, melted
- 2 tablespoons white sugar

Filling:

- 1 pound whipped cream cheese
- ¾ cup sugar
- 2 large eggs eggs
- 1 teaspoon vanilla extract

Topping:

- 1 (21 ounce) can cherry pie filling

Directions

Step 1

Preheat oven to 350 degrees F (175 degrees C). Line 24 muffin cups with foil liners.

Step 2

Mix graham cracker crumbs, melted butter, and 2 tablespoons sugar together in a bowl. Press crumbs into the bottoms of prepared muffin cups.

Step 3

Beat cream cheese, 3/4 cup sugar, eggs, and vanilla extract together in a bowl until filling is smooth. Divide filling between muffin cups.

Step 4

Bake in the preheated oven until top is golden around the edges and slightly cracked, about 10 minutes. Cool completely and top each with cherry pie filling.

Nutrition Facts

Per Serving:

182 calories; protein 1.8g 4% DV; carbohydrates 17.9g 6% DV; fat 11.9g 18% DV; cholesterol 48.5mg 16% DV; sodium 152.3mg 6% DV.

Creamy Chocolate Cupcakes

Prep: 20 mins **Cook:** 25 mins **Total:** 45 mins

Servings: 18

Yield: 18 cupcakes

Ingredients

- 1 ½ cups all-purpose flour
- 1 cup white sugar
- ¼ cup unsweetened cocoa powder
- 1 teaspoon baking soda
- ½ teaspoon salt
- 2 large eggs eggs, beaten
- ¾ cup water
- ½ cup vegetable oil
- 1 tablespoon apple cider vinegar
- 1 teaspoon Mexican vanilla extract
- 1 (8 ounce) package cream cheese, softened
- ⅓ cup white sugar
- ⅛ teaspoon salt
- 1 cup semisweet chocolate chips
- 1 cup chopped walnuts

Directions

Step 1

Preheat oven to 350 degrees F (175 degrees C). Line 18 muffin cups with paper cupcake liners.

Step 2

Mix flour, 1 cup sugar, cocoa powder, baking soda, and 1/2 teaspoon salt in a large mixing bowl. Add eggs, water, vegetable oil, vinegar, and vanilla extract; mix well. Pour batter into prepared muffin cups.

Step 3

Beat cream cheese, 1/3 cup sugar, and 1/8 teaspoon salt together in a separate bowl with an electric hand mixer until the sugar is fully incorporated into the cream cheese. Fold chocolate chips into the cheese mixture. Drop by tablespoonfuls into center of each cupcake; sprinkle with walnuts.

Step 4

Bake in preheated oven until a toothpick inserted into the middle of a cupcake comes out clean, 25 to 30 minutes. Cool in the pans for 10 minutes before removing to cool completely on a wire rack.

Nutrition Facts

Per Serving:

291 calories; protein 4.3g 9% DV; carbohydrates 30.6g 10% DV; fat 18.3g 28% DV; cholesterol 34.4mg 12% DV; sodium 197.3mg 8% DV.

Strawberry Cupcakes

Prep: 15 mins **Cook:** 20 mins **Additional:** 1 hr **Total:** 1 hr 35 mins

Servings: 12

Yield: 1 dozen cupcakes

Ingredients

- 10 tablespoons butter, room temperature
- ¾ cup white sugar
- 3 large eggs eggs
- 1 teaspoon strawberry extract
- 1 ¾ cups self-rising flour
- ¼ teaspoon salt
- ¼ cup finely chopped fresh strawberries, drained

Directions

Step 1

Preheat the oven to 325 degrees F (165 degrees C). Grease 12 cupcake pan cups or line with paper liners.

Step 2

In a large bowl, cream together the butter and sugar until light and fluffy. Beat in the eggs one at a time, then stir in the strawberry extract. Combine the self-rising flour and salt; stir into the batter just until blended. Fold in strawberries last. Spoon the batter into the prepared cups, dividing evenly.

Step 3

Bake in the preheated oven until the tops spring back when lightly pressed, 20 to 25 minutes. Cool in the pan set over a wire rack. When cool, arrange the cupcakes on a serving platter. Frost with desired frosting.

Nutrition Facts

Per Serving:

218 calories; protein 3.5g 7% DV; carbohydrates 26.4g 9% DV; fat 11g 17% DV; cholesterol 71.9mg 24% DV; sodium 365.7mg 15% DV.

Black Forest Cupcakes

Prep: 35 mins **Cook:** 12 mins **Additional:** 25 mins **Total:** 1 hr 12 mins

Servings: 24

Yield: 2 dozen

Ingredients

- 1 cup butter, softened
- 1 cup white sugar
- 4 large eggs eggs
- ¼ cup milk

- 1 ¼ cups all-purpose flour
- 6 tablespoons unsweetened cocoa powder
- 1 teaspoon baking soda

Filling:

- 1 (12 ounce) jar black cherry jam
- Topping:
- 1 pint heavy whipping cream
- 2 tablespoons sucralose sweetener (such as Splenda), or to taste

- 1 teaspoon vanilla extract
- 1 (6 ounce) jar maraschino cherries
- ½ cup grated milk chocolate, or to taste

Directions

Step 1

Preheat oven to 375 degrees F (190 degrees C). Line two muffin tins with cupcake liners.

Step 2

Beat butter and sugar in a large bowl until light and fluffy. Beat in eggs one at a time. Mix in milk. Add flour, cocoa powder, and baking soda; beat until batter is smooth.

Step 3

Pour batter into prepared muffin tins, filling each liner about half-full.

Step 4

Bake in the preheated oven until a toothpick inserted into the center comes out clean, 12 to 15 minutes. Transfer to a wire rack to cool completely, about 25 minutes.

Step 5

Cut tops off the cooled cupcakes. Remove a small amount of the center of each cupcake. Fill the centers with a small dab of black cherry jam. Put the tops back on, covering the jam.

Step 6

Combine heavy cream, sucralose sweetener, and vanilla extract in a large bowl. Whip until soft peaks form. Place in the refrigerator until chilled.

Step 7

Place whipped cream in a piping bag fitted with a round or star tip. Frost each cupcake with a swirl of whipped cream. Top each one with a maraschino cherry and grated chocolate.

Cook's Notes:

Use sugar in place of Splenda(R), if desired. I find that the whipped cream holds up longer in the fridge when I use sucralose.

If you don't have a piping bag, you can cut the corner off a resealable plastic bag and slip the piping tip into the corner.

Nutrition Facts

Per Serving:

275 calories; protein 2.9g 6% DV; carbohydrates 29g 9% DV; fat 17.3g 27% DV; cholesterol 79.6mg 27% DV; sodium 132.3mg 5% DV.

Champagne Cupcakes

Prep: 15 mins **Cook:** 20 mins **Additional:** 40 mins **Total:** 1 hr 15 mins

Servings: 24

Yield: 2 dozen cupcakes

Ingredients

- cooking spray
- 1 (18.25 ounce) package white cake mix
- 1 ¼ cups Champagne or other sparkling white wine at room temperature
- ⅓ cup vegetable oil
- 3 large eggs eggs
- ½ cup butter, softened
- 4 cups confectioners' sugar
- ¼ cup Champagne or other sparkling white wine at room temperature
- 1 teaspoon vanilla extract

Directions

Step 1

Preheat oven to 350 degrees F (175 degrees C).

Step 2

Spray 24 muffin cups with cooking spray.

Step 3

Mix cake mix and 1 1/4 cup Champagne in a large mixing bowl; stir in vegetable oil and eggs. Beat batter with an electric mixer on medium speed for 2 minutes.

Step 4

Pour batter into the prepared muffin cups, filling them 3/4 full.

Step 5

Bake cupcakes in the preheated oven until a toothpick inserted into the middle of a cupcake comes out clean, about 20 minutes.

Step 6

Cool cupcakes in pans for 10 minutes before removing to finish cooling, about 30 more minutes.

Step 7

Mix butter, 1 cup confectioners' sugar, 1/4 cup Champagne, and vanilla extract in a bowl. Stir in remaining confectioners' sugar, 1 cup at a time, until frosting is smooth and creamy. Spread on cooled cupcakes.

Cook's Note:

You don't have to use expensive champagne - the cheap stuff works great! These are perfect for New Year's Eve and weddings!

Nutrition Facts

Per Serving:

256 calories; protein 1.8g 4% DV; carbohydrates 37.9g 12% DV; fat 9.9g 15% DV; cholesterol 33.4mg 11% DV; sodium 178.4mg 7% DV.

Cream Filled Chocolate Cupcakes

Prep: 40 mins **Cook:** 20 mins **Additional:** 30 mins **Total:** 1 hr 30 mins

Servings: 24

Yield: 2 dozen cupcakes

Ingredients

- 2 ½ cups all-purpose flour
- 2 cups white sugar
- ⅓ cup unsweetened cocoa powder
- 1 teaspoon baking powder
- ¼ teaspoon salt
- 1 cup vegetable oil
- 1 cup buttermilk
- 2 large eggs eggs
- 1 teaspoon vanilla extract
- 2 teaspoons baking soda
- 1 cup hot water
- ⅔ cup shortening
- ½ cup white sugar
- ⅓ cup milk
- 1 tablespoon water
- 1 teaspoon vanilla extract
- ¼ teaspoon salt
- ½ cup confectioners' sugar

Directions

Step 1

Preheat oven to 350 degrees F (175 degrees C). Grease two 12-cup muffin tins.

Step 2

Sift flour, 2 cups white sugar, cocoa powder, baking powder, and salt together in a large bowl. Beat vegetable oil, buttermilk, eggs, and 1 teaspoon vanilla extract into the flour mixture using an electric hand mixer on medium until smooth, about 3 minutes.

Step 3

Stir baking soda and hot water together in a small bowl; mix into batter. Pour batter into muffin cups to 2/3 full.

Step 4

Bake in the preheated oven until a toothpick inserted in the center of a cupcake comes out clean, about 20 minutes. Cool in the pans for 10 minutes before removing to cool completely on a wire rack.

Step 5

Beat shortening, 1/2 cup white sugar, milk, 1 tablespoon water, 1 teaspoon vanilla extract, and salt together in a bowl using an electric hand mixer until smooth, 5 to 7 minutes. Add confectioners' sugar; beat until fully incorporated, 3 to 5 minutes.

Step 6

Insert frosting into cupcakes using a pastry tube fitted with a rosette tip. Frost the tops of cupcakes with remaining frosting.

Nutrition Facts

Per Serving:

284 calories; protein 2.6g 5% DV; carbohydrates 34.8g 11% DV; fat 15.6g 24% DV; cholesterol 16.2mg 5% DV; sodium 192.5mg 8% DV.

Grownup Chai Chocolate Cupcakes

Prep: 15 mins **Cook:** 30 mins **Total:** 45 mins

Servings: 10

Yield: 10 cupcakes

Ingredients

- ½ cup unsalted butter
- 2 (1 ounce) squares unsweetened chocolate, chopped
- 4 eaches chai tea bags
- ½ cup all-purpose flour, sifted
- ¾ cup white sugar
- 2 large eggs eggs
- 1 teaspoon vanilla extract

Directions

Step 1

Preheat oven to 325 degrees F (165 degrees C). Line a muffin tin with 10 paper liners.

Step 2

Melt butter and chocolate in the top of a double boiler over simmering water until smooth, stirring frequently and scraping down the sides with a rubber spatula to avoid scorching, 5 to 10 minutes.

Step 3

Open tea bags and pour the chai mixture into a spice grinder; grind into a fine powder, 5 to 10 seconds.

Step 4

Mix flour, sugar, and chai powder together in a large bowl; add eggs, one at a time, whisking until batter is smooth after each addition. Stir in vanilla extract. Pour chocolate mixture into batter, stirring until just combined. Pour batter into the prepared muffin cups.

Step 5

Bake in the preheated oven until a toothpick inserted in the center of a muffin comes out clean and the tops are glossy and slightly cracked, about 25 minutes. Remove muffins immediately from tin and cool on a wire rack.

Cook's Note:

Different brands of tea spice their chai differently, you may need another tea bag or two if your tea is mildly spiced. The flavor should be noticeable but not overpowering.

Nutrition Facts

Per Serving:

207 calories; protein 2.7g 5% DV; carbohydrates 21.8g 7% DV; fat 13.2g 20% DV; cholesterol 61.6mg 21% DV; sodium 16.8mg 1% DV.

Chocolate Chai Cupcakes

Prep: 25 mins **Cook:** 15 mins **Total:** 40 mins

Servings: 6

Yield: 6 cupcakes

Ingredients

- 6 tablespoons nonfat dry milk powder
- ¾ cup hot black tea, or as needed
- nonstick cooking spray with flour
- 2 teaspoons ground cinnamon
- 1 teaspoon ground nutmeg
- 1 teaspoon ground allspice
- ½ teaspoon ground cloves
- ¼ teaspoon ground black pepper
- 1 cup all-purpose flour
- 1 cup lightly packed brown sugar
- 6 tablespoons unsweetened cocoa powder
- 1 teaspoon baking soda
- ½ teaspoon baking powder
- ½ teaspoon salt
- ¼ cup sunflower seed oil
- 1 egg, lightly beaten
- 1 teaspoon grated fresh ginger

Directions

Step 1

Put nonfat milk powder in a measuring cup; stir in enough black tea to make 1 cup. Stir until milk is dissolved. Set aside to cool.

Step 2

Preheat oven to 375 degrees F (190 degrees C). Spray a muffin pan with nonstick cooking spray.

Step 3

Combine cinnamon, nutmeg, allspice, cloves, and black pepper together in a small bowl.

Step 4

Sift spice mixture, flour, brown sugar, cocoa powder, baking soda, baking powder, and salt together into a large bowl. Stir cooled tea mixture, oil, and egg into flour mixture until batter is just combined; fold in ginger. Spoon batter into the prepared muffin cups, filling each 3/4-full.

Step 5

Bake in the preheated oven until a toothpick inserted in the center of a cupcake comes out clean, 12 to 15 minutes. Cool cupcakes on wire racks.

Cook's Note:

The subtle flavors are better experienced without additional frosting. Enjoy one with a cup of chai!

Use English breakfast or Darjeeling tea for the black tea.

Nutrition Facts

Per Serving:

305 calories; protein 6.9g 14% DV; carbohydrates 47.9g 16% DV; fat 11.1g 17% DV; cholesterol 28.8mg 10% DV; sodium 504.2mg 20% DV.

Pink Lemonade Cupcakes with Pink Buttercream Frosting

Prep: 20 mins **Cook:** 20 mins **Total:** 40 mins

Servings: 12

Yield: 1 dozen cupcakes

Ingredients

Cupcakes:

- ½ cup white sugar
- ¼ cup vegetable oil
- ¼ cup cold water
- 2 large eggs eggs
- 3 tablespoons pink lemonade powder

- ⅓ cup buttermilk
- 1 cup all-purpose flour
- ½ teaspoon baking soda
- ½ teaspoon baking powder
- 1 dash red food coloring, or as desired

Buttercream Frosting:

- 4 ½ cups confectioners' sugar
- ½ cup unsalted butter, at room temperature
- ¼ cup half-and-half

- 2 tablespoons pink lemonade powder
- 1 dash red food coloring, or as desired

Directions

Step 1

Preheat oven to 350 degrees F (175 degrees C). Line 12 muffin cups with paper liners.

Step 2

Whisk white sugar, oil, water, eggs, and 3 tablespoons pink lemonade powder together in a bowl; stir in buttermilk until smooth. Whisk flour, baking soda, and baking powder together in a separate bowl; beat into sugar mixture just until batter is combined. Add just enough food coloring to turn batter pink. Spoon batter into muffin cups.

Step 3

Bake in the preheated oven until cupcakes spring back when lightly touched, 20 to 25 minutes.

Step 4

Beat confectioners' sugar, butter, half-and-half, and 2 tablespoons pink lemonade powder together in a bowl using an electric mixer until frosting is smooth and creamy. Add enough food coloring to make a pink frosting; spread onto cupcakes.

Cook's Note:

Whole milk can be substituted for the half-and-half, if desired.

Nutrition Facts

Per Serving:

404 calories; protein 2.6g 5% DV; carbohydrates 69.4g 22% DV; fat 13.8g 21% DV; cholesterol 53.5mg 18% DV; sodium 96.8mg 4% DV.

www.ingramcontent.com/pod-product-compliance
Lightning Source LLC
Chambersburg PA
CBHW080903160726
48000CB00009B/2836